D1377612

"*Should FDR have sought a fourth term? Matthew B. Wills, attorney turned historian, offers an answer that you'll read with horrified fascination. Be prepared as, item by item, Wills lays out his evidence and builds an utterly damning case. This is NOT an anti-FDR book, but rather a fair and objective analysis of the effects Roosevelt's poor health was having upon his relationships—personal and political— upon his energy and upon his judgment during the final months of World War II.*"

—C. BRIAN KELLY, military author and former
editor-in-chief of *World War II* magazine and *Military
History* magazine.

"*It may be thought that everything possible has been written about Franklin Roosevelt, but Matthew Wills' book provides a welcome addition to the literature. Sensitively and fairly, Wills delves into the president's mounting frailties and how they affected both American policy and the outcome of World War II. Like the author's previous work on Harry Hopkins, this is an important contribution to our knowledge of the war that made us what we are today.*"

—RICHARD M. LANGWORTH, CBE,
Chairman, Board of Trustees, The Churchill Center

"*Matthew B. Wills answered to my satisfaction why President Roosevelt did so little to discourage or attempt to prevent Stalin from taking over control of post-war Poland and ultimately all of Eastern Europe. He was too ill and exhausted from a serious heart condition to make the necessary effort to counter Stalin's actions which were the opposite of his avowed pledges to live in harmony with his war-time allies.*

President Roosevelt's official doctor alleged [from] 1944 to April 1945—and even after the president's death—that his heart was in good shape and his health was good. The story of how we know the president was deathly ill makes exciting reading and raises the immediate question of what can be done to prevent a similar catastrophe in the future."

—DR. BERYL SPRINKEL, former Cabinet member,
Chairman of the Council of Economic Advisors

"Mr. Wills' book is fascinating in its delineation of the relationships between FDR, Stalin, Churchill, Truman and the big city political bosses who secured his nomination as V.P., as well as Jimmy Byrnes, [Harold] Ickes, Harry Hopkins, Stilwell and other key figures in World War II. The very dramatic deterioration in FDR's health in 1943 and '44 had such serious ramifications for the post–World War II world, as he became unable to deal with Stalin and unable properly to support Churchill.

From a physician's point of view, it is disturbing to read about the incompetence of his White House physician and the medical dissembling involving family and key figures in the Executive Branch.

We owe Senator Birch Bayh and the honorable Herbert Brownell a great debt of gratitude for authoring the 25th amendment that now makes obfuscation regarding the president's health a virtual impossibility. The role of Physician to the President remains vital to the success of the amendment, but that White House position is frequently not appointed, and it was not under President Clinton.

Even as a fourteen-year-old boy in 1944, I was extremely aware of how sick FDR had become when the nation elected him to a fourth term. It is remarkable how his health was disregarded in the FDR White House and in the election, but not at all surprising. Mr. Wills describes it all in intimate detail and in very personal terms."

—DR. BURTON J. LEE III, physician to President
George Herbert Walker Bush

"In March 1944, a confidential medical examination of Franklin Roosevelt revealed a dying president. Eleven years of leading the nation through the Great Depression and then world war had taken a terrible toll. Those close to Roosevelt might have kept the details of his illness—congestive heart failure—from the public, but his rapidly deteriorating condition was certainly evident to his advisors and anyone who saw those shocking photographs from Yalta. In 1944, with a campaign for a fourth term looming, the war not yet won and the seeds of the Cold War already germinating, was FDR in any condition to negotiate with the likes of Joseph Stalin, or perform any of the other demanding duties of his office? Matthew B. Wills' study of 'the diminished president' during his last years answers many of these questions."

—JAN K. HERMAN, historian for the Navy
Medical Department

A DIMINISHED PRESIDENT

FDR IN 1944

A DIMINISHED PRESIDENT

FDR IN 1944

Matthew B. Wills

PUBLISHED BY IVY HOUSE PUBLISHING GROUP
5122 Bur Oak Circle, Raleigh, NC 27612
United States of America
919-782-0281
www.ivyhousebooks.com

ISBN: 1-57197-347-8
Library of Congress Control Number: 2002113068

Printed in the United States of America

to the memory of
Ensign Philip Henry Ryan Jr., United States Navy

and to
Julia Ryan Wills

two Virginians of undoubted grace

By the same author:

Wartime Missions of Harry L. Hopkins

TABLE OF CONTENTS

Foreword xi

Acknowledgments xiii

Chapter One - Prologue 1

Chapter Two - A Year of Growing Concern 17

Chapter Three - The Selection of Truman 35

Chapter Four - Hopkins and Roosevelt 51

Chapter Five - Churchill and Roosevelt 67

Chapter Six - The Sacrifice of Stilwell 91

Chapter Seven - Hull, Roosevelt and the
    Failure of American Foreign Policy 117

Chapter Eight - Epilogue 147

Source Notes 157

Bibliography 171

Index 179

FOREWORD

The fact that Franklin Roosevelt was ill for months before his last term in office as president of the United States is a matter of history. It might not be so universally accepted as history were it not for Dr. Howard Bruenn, a young commander in the Navy Medical Corps, who, in 1944, served at the Bethesda Naval Hospital as Roosevelt's personal physician under the command of Admiral Ross McIntire. McIntire clearly believed that any negative information about the president's health should be kept not only from the American people but from anyone and everyone—and indeed from Roosevelt himself. And that is how it was then.

I first met Howard Bruenn at West Chop on Martha's Vineyard in the summer of 1942. He was married to Dorothy Conner, the best friend of one of my best friends, Mary Peltz, whom I would one day marry. They had known Howard as a doctor at the Columbia Presbyterian Hospital in New York City when they were nurses in training.

My first impression of Dr. Bruenn was of an attractive and very bright young doctor. He was also, as I remember him, modest and soft spoken. The thought that he was on the way to making an impact on American history did not occur to me and would not, I believe, have occurred to any of his contemporaries in the early days of World War II. If, however, in his ongoing naval career as Roosevelt's heart specialist beginning in March 1944, his findings had not been kept secret, his name today would be better known and U.S. history might have been different.

An example of this secrecy occurred in Bethesda in 1944. My wife, Mary, in 1944 was married to Dr. Theodore Russell, an old friend and colleague of Howard Bruenn. Dr. Russell was also at the Bethesda Naval Hospital, although not a cardiologist. Mary remembers a morning while playing with her three-year-old daughter, watching a khaki-clad naval officer walking toward the house. His mission was to make it very clear that if any information about the medical findings in connection with the president's illness were not kept totally secret, a change of duty for Dr. Russell could result—a warning not to be taken lightly. At the same time the Washington papers stated that Roosevelt was suffering from a mild respiratory illness and was a patient at the Bethesda Naval Hospital.

In this book, Matthew Wills shows that FDR's treatment of Byrnes, Wallace, Truman, Hopkins, Churchill and Stilwell was marked by lapses in judgment that almost certainly were related to medical conditions discovered by Dr. Bruenn but kept secret by the orders of Admiral McIntire.

The last time I saw Howard Bruenn was in 1994 in his home in Riverdale, New York, a year before he died. He was failing physically, but was completely undimmed intellectually. Surprisingly to me, he didn't discuss any of the events and relationships that make *A Diminished President* so fascinating. Rather, he took great pleasure in producing a number of mementos of the war years, including a 1945 autographed photograph of Joseph Stalin, whom he regarded personally as a friendly and unique leader who took advantage of Roosevelt's increasing vulnerability and weakness.

Matthew Wills' previous book, *Wartime Missions of Harry L. Hopkins,* is a clear promise that what you are about to read in *A Diminished President—FDR in 1944* will be factually impeccable, historically illuminating, and a deeply engrossing and rewarding experience.

—Lewis Perry, Jr.
Colorado Springs
Headmaster Emeritus
Fountain Valley School

ACKNOWLEDGMENTS

Before I started writing history, I was engaged in the practice of law. That background has undoubtedly benefited me in my present endeavors. Hardy Cross Dillard of the Law School at the University of Virginia was unforgettable. I will always remember his description of Gertrude Stein as she lay dying. A friend asked her, "What is the answer?" She paused and replied, "What is the question?" Like the lawyer, the historian must grapple with the question before he can ever get to the answer. As a young lawyer, my greatest mentor was Frederick T. Henry, who was the city attorney for Colorado Springs for many years. Outwardly modest and shy, he had a gift for unerring analysis. He painstakingly examined all sides of a case before rendering his opinion. His example has stood me in good stead.

The disposition I have toward history preceded law school by many years. My father, Jesse Ely Wills, was a businessman, but he was also a poet and a bibliophile. To my father I credit my love of books. It was he who introduced me to Churchill. Without his guidance I might never have read *The Gathering Storm, Their Finest*

Hour, The Grand Alliance, The Hinge of Fate, Closing the Ring, and *Triumph and Tragedy,* which remain the most moving works of history I have ever read.

During World War II, our parents sent my brother, Ridley, and me to a summer camp in the mountains of North Carolina. Robert K. Massie was one of the counselors. In August 1945, shortly after the Japanese surrender, Massie and I sat up all night on a railroad car that was slowly carrying us back to our homes in Nashville. He spoke to me about the war, the new weapon that could conceivably destroy civilization, and the post-war world with all its uncertainties. I was twelve years old, and I had never participated in a conversation like that in my entire life. Long before Massie achieved distinction at Yale and Oxford, and long before he went on to fame as a writer, he had already influenced my life. His first book, *Nicholas and Alexandra,* is still my favorite one-volume history. It gave me an enormous appreciation for the human side of history.

Writing a work of history is never a solitary experience. With gratitude, I want to acknowledge all of those who gave their time, their suggestions and their encouragement.

One such person who gave his support is Lewis Perry Jr., a graduate of Harvard College and Oxford University. In World War II he served as an officer on the U.S.S. *Santee,* an escort carrier that was both torpedoed by a submarine and hit by a kamikaze airplane in the course of a few hours during the Battle of Leyte Gulf. After the war, he had a long and distinguished career in education, first as a master at the Lawrenceville School and then for twenty years as headmaster at the Fountain Valley School. I am truly honored that he has written the foreword to my book.

Lewis Perry's wife, Mary, introduced me to her lifelong friend, Dorothy Bruenn. This proved to be a wonderful introduction both professionally and personally. Dorothy Bruenn's husband, Howard, was a cardiologist, who, for slightly more than a year, had the task of looking after the most famous president of the twentieth century. Some twenty-five years after Franklin Roosevelt's death he published the first definitive article on Roosevelt's final illness. Dorothy generously gave me a copy of this article, a copy of a 1990 interview between her husband and a Navy historian, and a letter to her husband from Vice Admiral Ross T. McIntire, of which otherwise I would never have known . She also shared her recollections of that long ago era. I will always be grateful to Mary Perry for putting me in touch with her friend and for her kind assistance and friendship.

Jan Herman is the navy historian who interviewed Dr. Bruenn in 1990. Mr. Herman has spent more than ten years delving into the suspicious circumstances surrounding the disappearance of President Roosevelt's medical records. He has generously shared his research with me, and I will always be grateful to him.

To write with accuracy about Franklin Roosevelt's heart condition presented some challenges; however, I was able to compensate for my non-medical background by consulting with one of my closest friends, Dilworth P. Sellers. Dr. Sellers is both a distinguished cardiologist and a perceptive student of history. With great patience he answered my questions about the risks of congestive heart failure, a disease with which his own father was afflicted. In addition, he provided me with a number of medical articles dealing with President Roosevelt's illnesses. Finally, he reviewed my manuscript for medical errors. For his guidance, I am forever grateful.

Three other friends, who have given much thought to Franklin Roosevelt's presidency, have read my manuscript and given me the benefit of their comments. They are C. Brian Kelly, author and former editor-in-chief of *World War II Magazine;* George S. Wills, president of Wills & Associates, Inc., Public Affairs Counsel, whom I regrettably cannot claim as kinsman; Vincent Davis, formerly director of the Patterson School of Diplomacy and International Commerce. I am grateful to each of them.

It would have been virtually impossible to complete my research without the able assistance of the Franklin D. Roosevelt Library at Hyde Park, New York. As with my book on Harry L. Hopkins, Robert Parks of the FDR Library, an archivist par excellence, has extended his assistance throughout my research. I deeply appreciate his help and his unvarying courtesy.

I would also like to thank Donna Kwiatkowski, Terry Johansen, and earlier, Linda Addington, who struggled for weeks with my handwriting before producing a working manuscript. During the revision process, they forged ahead until they thought I was completely satisfied only to learn that I wanted yet another revision. I am grateful for each of them for their diligence, their competence, their patience and, above all, for their cheerful demeanor under all circumstances.

Our four children have observed their father striving to write his second book from afar. I am especially grateful to our daughter, Carter Wills McKenzie, for her scrutiny of the final manuscript in search of errata that her father had failed to catch. For their love and support, I am grateful.

This book is dedicated to my wife, Julia Ryan Wills, and to the memory of her only brother, Philip, a graduate of the Naval Academy, who lost his life at twenty-three in a flight training accident. Her contributions to this book, though indirect, are profound. It is the historian's task to write retrospectively about the human condition with candor and compassion. Sometimes I need to be reminded about compassion. Julia has quietly done so by her example. For that, and for her support and her love, I am eternally grateful.

CHAPTER ONE

Prologue

To write anything about Franklin D. Roosevelt is a daunting task. The Franklin Delano Roosevelt Library alone has over 44,000 books covering the life and times of Franklin and Eleanor Roosevelt. The authors of these volumes include the most distinguished writers of the last century. It might seem that no aspect of this man's public or private life has escaped scrutiny; nevertheless, a steady stream of books on FDR continues to appear every year.

This president was not easily understood by either his family or his closest associates. His eldest son, James, once wrote, "Nowhere in the world really was there anyone for him with whom he could unlock his mind and his thoughts. Politics, domestic economy, war strategy, post-war planning he could talk over with dozens of persons. Of what was inside him, of what really drove him, Father talked with no one."[1] Secretary of Labor Frances Perkins, the first woman to be appointed to a Cabinet office, remembered Roosevelt as "the most complicated human being I ever knew."[2] Robert E. Sherwood, the playwright, who served Roosevelt as a speech writer, agreed with the Madam Secretary. In his classic work, *Roosevelt and Hopkins,* published three years after Roosevelt's death, Sherwood concluded, "Being a writer by trade, I tried continually to study him, to try to look beyond his charming and amusing and warmly affectionate surface into his heavily forested interior. But I could never really understand what was going on in there."[3]

Many historians have ranked Franklin Roosevelt as the second greatest American president, behind only Lincoln. He is almost certainly the greatest president of the twentieth century. He was confronted with the gravest crises (besides the Civil War) in America's history—the Great Depression and World War II. If he had been president during more tranquil times, his place in history inevitably would have been lower.

In the prime of life, Roosevelt was stricken with poliomyelitis. While he survived, his lower limbs were rendered almost useless. Most men would have given up, dropped their ambitions and taken the course of least resistance. Roosevelt's mother, whom he adored, urged him to become a gentleman farmer on her Dutchess County estate. After a few years of lassitude, he reentered politics. In 1928, he was elected governor of New York. Four years later, he was elected president of the United States.

The generation which came of age in the 1990s can scarcely conceive of the chaos and despair which gripped America sixty years earlier. In 1932, the Dow Jones Industrial Average hit a new low of forty-eight dollars, down from a high for the year of only eighty-eight dollars. The GNP was minus 23 percent. Unemployment had reached 23.6 percent. These cold statistics hardly reveal the full extent of human misery. *Fortune Magazine* described the plight of men out of work with telling words, "Men who lost their jobs dropped out of sight. They were quiet and you had to know just when and where to find them; at night, for instance, on the edge of town huddling for warmth around a bonfire, or even the municipal incinerator; at dawn, picking over the garbage dump for scraps of food or salvageable clothing."[4]

Roosevelt's courage, determination, and his abiding faith in a divine destiny for his country and for himself had enthralled the American people at a time when they were fast losing faith in themselves, their leaders and their institutions. His first inaugural address was awesome. A single sentence from that speech has now become a permanent part of the national ethos, "So, first of all, let me assert my firm belief that the only thing we have to fear is fear itself—nameless, unreasoning, unjustified terror which paralyzes needed efforts to convert retreat into advance."[5]

On March 4, 1933, the day of his inauguration as president, Franklin Roosevelt was thirty-three days past his fifty-first birthday. Because of his bout with poliomyelitis, then a dread disease, he and his political advisors had taken the unusual step of releasing information about his general health well in advance of the 1932 election. Among the selective medical details given to the press were two that, in hindsight, appear somewhat ominous. At the time of his pre-election medical examination, his blood pressure was 140/100, somewhat elevated over the norm for his age of 120/80. In addition, his electrocardiogram showed an abnormal heart tracing that indicated an enlargement of the left side of the heart.

From the standpoint of clinical observations and laboratory tests, this medical report fell short of a definitive statement of Roosevelt's condition in 1932; nevertheless, it was never challenged. Neither the press nor the medical profession nor the Republican Party showed any real interest in this aspect of Roosevelt's health. His much more obvious health problem was the permanent paralysis of his lower limbs. His plight was well known to the American people, who largely viewed it as the saga of a heroic man who had overcome enormous adversity to achieve the highest office in the land. FDR was never content to let the facts of his paralysis speak for themselves. This led him to go to extraordinary lengths to conceal that he was dependent on a wheelchair. The truth was that he used one every day except when he was bedridden. Roosevelt strictly forbade any photographs of himself in a wheelchair. It is believed that there are only two photographs in existence of FDR sitting in a wheelchair. They were both taken at the president's mother's estate near Hyde Park by an individual whom he trusted implicitly. She kept them in her exclusive possession for the remainder of Roosevelt's life.

President Roosevelt's medical records covering his first two terms are virtually nonexistent. Following his death in April 1945, his personal physician, Ross T. McIntire, wrote a memoir which included some unremarkable comments on the president's general health from 1936 through most of 1943. Regarding his health in 1937, at the beginning of his second term, he wrote, "Although he was a bit too heavy, weighing around 190, every check showed him organically sound."[6] Of his condition five years later, shortly after Pearl Harbor, McIntire gave an equally favorable summary: "There was an attack of the influenza in 1941, but he recovered rapidly, and regular examinations showed no cause for worry. The kidney and liver functioned normally, the blood picture stayed on a good level, and cardiovascular measurements stayed on a good level."[7] McIntire assured his readers that after the Teheran Conference in November, 1943, ". . . my examinations at the close of the conference found him so fit, both mentally and physically, that I did not think it necessary to urge any change in the exacting itinerary that had been mapped out."[8]

It is now known that the president had congestive heart failure during at least the last twelve months of his life. McIntire had never suspected this condition before March 1944, when the president was examined by a young navy cardiologist, Howard G. Bruenn. How long the president had this disease is unknown. From 1932 through the remainder of Roosevelt's life, the only drug available that could partially control its most serious symptoms was digitalis. Congestive heart failure means that the heart is unable to pump enough blood to supply the rest of the body adequately. In addition to impeding heart function, congestive heart failure puts a severe strain on other organs, especially the lungs and the kidneys. Even with modern medicine, this disease still kills half of those who have it within five years of its detection.

The most effective preventive measures against this disease are keeping blood pressure and blood cholesterol at safe levels, controlling body weight, staying fit and not smoking. Unfortunately for President Roosevelt, an understanding of these measures lay far in the future. Before 1944, the ravages of cardiovascular disease were not yet apparent. Thereafter a different story emerges. There is no precise cause-and-effect relationship between a president's health and any of the greater or lesser decisions that any president must make; nevertheless, any medical condition that impairs a president's capacity carries grave risks for the nation. In an extreme situation, it is obvious that a president should not be making any important decisions. Providentially, throughout the twentieth century, the United States had been spared that particular crisis save once. After President Woodrow Wilson's collapse in Colorado in September 1919, followed by a thrombosis in Washington on October 2, he was no longer fit to perform his duties. Roosevelt's impairment was much less serious than Wilson's; nevertheless, in 1944, the indisputable decline in his health more than likely caused him to exercise his judgment in ways that were uncharacteristically petulant, superficial or shortsighted.

That year the president aided and abetted corrupt "big city bosses" in eliminating all candidates for vice president except for the one candidate whom the bosses wanted. That year he distanced himself from his old friend, Harry L. Hopkins, who had been perhaps his most astute advisor. That year he provoked Winston Churchill in ways that were often invidious and sometimes devious. That year he sacked a renowned four-star general, Joseph W. Stilwell, in order to placate Generalissimo Chiang Kai-shek, who was leading China to disaster. That year he ignored the reality that Stalin planned to subjugate Poland and most of Eastern Europe. Individually and collectively, his actions reveal a sadly diminished president; however, in order to put them in perspective, it is essential to examine the state of Franklin Roosevelt's health. It is now established beyond any reasonable doubt that FDR's health was failing. But to what extent was it failing? And if it was failing drastically, how did that affect his decisions? There is no easy answer to the last question; but it is a question that cannot be avoided.

FDR in 1933, age 51, his first year as president.

FDR in 1934, age 52.

FDR in 1935, age 53.

FDR in 1936, age 54.

FDR in 1937, age 55, the first year of his second term.

FDR in 1938, age 56.

FDR in 1939, age 57.

FDR in 1940, age 58. This is one of only two photographs known to exist of President Roosevelt in a wheelchair.

FDR in 1941, age 59, the first year of his third term.

FDR in 1942, age 60.

FDR in 1943, age 61.

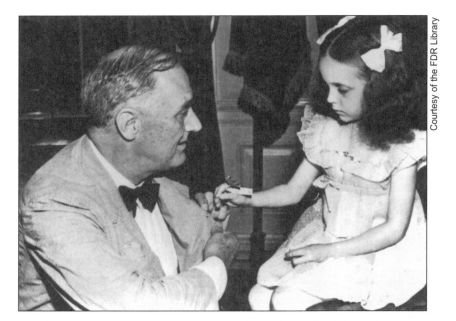

An ill and weary FDR in 1944 receiving a flower for his lapel from the young daughter of a serviceman.

Sometime in 1944.

Wednesday, July 26, 1944, FDR on board the heavy cruiser U.S.S. *Baltimore* at Pearl Harbor with General Douglas MacArthur and Admiral Chester Nimitz.

Tuesday, September 12, 1944. FDR with Churchill on the terrace of the Citadel, Quebec.

Saturday, October 21, 1944. FDR campaigning in Manhattan seventeen days before his election to a fourth term.

FDR in 1944, age 62. Unknown to the public, his health was failing drastically.

CHAPTER TWO

A Year of Growing Concern

"Yet none of us was warned that Father's life might be in danger."
JAMES ROOSEVELT, THE PRESIDENT'S ELDEST SON

December 31, 1943, was for America the third New Year's Eve of the war. The president was satisfied with the progress of the war, but neither he nor anyone else knew when the fighting would end. He was hardly in the mood for an extravagant New Year's Eve party, but he did invite some immediate family and a few intimate friends to join Mrs. Roosevelt and himself for eggnog and dessert. Around 11:30, they all gathered in the president's upstairs study. The group included Bishop Atwood, an old friend of the family and the former Episcopal Bishop of Arizona, Secretary of the Treasury Henry Morgenthau Jr. and his wife, Elinor, Anna Roosevelt Boettiger, the Roosevelts' only daughter, Malvina Thompson, Mrs. Roosevelt's secretary, Mrs. Harold Pratt, a friend of Mrs. Roosevelt, and Margaret

Suckley, a close friend and distant relative of the president, plus three Roosevelt grandchildren.

President Roosevelt entered from his adjoining bedroom wearing a white bathrobe. He was seated on the end of the upright sofa to the right of the fireplace. Mrs. Roosevelt appeared in a voluminous black silk dress and a black lace scarf. A few minutes before midnight, they joined in singing "Auld Lang Syne." Then, with cups of eggnog in their hands, they waited for the radio to announce that the new year had arrived. The president was the first to speak. He said quietly, "Our first toast will be to the United States of America."[1] Henry Morgenthau, who was devoted to the president, made the next toast, "The President of the United States, God bless him."[2] It seemed more like a prayer than a toast. It was more apt than Morgenthau could have known.

President Roosevelt was then in the twelfth month of his sixty-second year. He had served as president for ten years, nine months and twenty-seven days, longer than any predecessor. At thirty-nine, his life had been irrevocably changed by poliomyelitis which largely deprived him of the use of his legs. Before polio, he had excelled at golf, tennis and sailing. He had not engaged in those sports or any other vigorous exercise for twenty-two years. He had become a heavy smoker, invariably using a cigarette holder. He always enjoyed the cocktail hour, when he consumed a moderate amount of alcohol. Like so many other Americans of that era, his "unvarying breakfast dish was ham or bacon and eggs."[3] His unhealthy lifestyle, coupled with the inevitable stress of his years in office, certainly did nothing to ward off the cardiovascular disease that would threaten his life before the end of March 1944.

The president's cardiovascular disease had been undetected before March 28, 1944. The person who had the primary responsibility for safeguarding the president's health was Vice Admiral Ross T. McIntire. He was both the president's personal physician and the Surgeon General of the Navy. McIntire, a native of Oregon, had practiced medicine in that state for five years before joining the Medical Corps of the Navy as an assistant surgeon with the rank of Lieutenant Junior Grade. By 1932, he had risen to Lieutenant Commander and was assigned to the Naval Hospital in Washington, with additional duties as instructor in ophthalmology and otolaryngology in the Naval Medical School. McIntire owed his appointment as White House Physician to the venerable Admiral Cary Grayson, who had been Woodrow Wilson's physician and an old friend of FDR. McIntire's new appointment escalated his Navy career. He was promoted to Commander in 1934. Only four years later, he attained the rank of Rear Admiral and became the Surgeon General of the Navy. McIntire was subsequently promoted to Vice Admiral.

McIntire reached his fifty-fifth birthday in August 1944. Of less than average height, he was overweight, with a round, almost flaccid face. His official photographs reveal a stern demeanor with a trace of self-importance. There is little doubt that McIntire reveled in his positions as Surgeon General of the Navy, as President Roosevelt's personal physician, and as a self-proclaimed member of "the intimate White House circle." Moreover, McIntire was never prone to understate his role in that circle. He wrote of his response to the attack on Pearl Harbor as follows:

> Going home, I was at luncheon when the White House operator gave me the news of Pearl Harbor and the President's request to report at once. Pa Watson (General Edwin M Watson, the president's appointment secretary) was in Charlottesville, and Admiral Leahy * could not be found; so Steve Early and I took over.[4]

McIntire described himself as "an eye, ear, nose and throat man,"[5] which may well have been the only field in which he was competent to practice medicine. Over his years as White House physician, McIntire's house calls followed a pattern. Around 8:30 every morning, he casually checked on the president. What interested him most were "the President's color, the tone of his voice, the tilt of his chin and the way he tackled his orange juice, cereal and eggs."[6] Promptly at 5:30 every afternoon, McIntire returned to the White House to check on the president. He routinely treated the president's chronic sinus problem with a spray containing adrenaline, which likely increased Roosevelt's blood pressure. Whenever the president left Washington on an extended trip, McIntire accompanied him.

Although McIntire would later write that "The President . . . never had any serious heart condition,"[7] in early 1943 he had placed restrictions on the maximum altitude that the president could fly. Roosevelt's very first flight as president took place in January 1943, when he flew to Casablanca by way of Brazil for a

---

* On December 7, 1941, Admiral William D. Leahy was in Vichy, France, where he was serving as ambassador to France under the wavering Pétain regime.

meeting with Churchill. Harry Hopkins, who attended all of the conferences with Churchill save one, kept notes which revealed McIntire's concern. "Dr. McIntire was worried about the President's bad heart—nothing happened—he slept for two hours after lunch. . . . McIntire heard that we had to fly over mountains 13,000 feet to get to our rendezvous with Churchill. Something will have to be done about that in the morning for the President can't stand that height."[8]

In 1944, the first medical problem to cause McIntire concern was influenza. Its lingering effects precluded the president from personally delivering the State of the Union message to Congress. In a fireside chat broadcast from the White House on January 11, he explained, "It has been my custom to deliver these annual messages in person, . . . but, like a great many other people, I have had the flu, and although I am practically recovered, my doctor simply would not let me leave the White House to go up to the Capitol."[9] McIntire has described the aftermath of the president's flu: "The attack hung on and finally left behind a nagging inflammation of the bronchial tubes. Coughing spells racked him by day and broke his rest at night. More disturbing than anything else, there was the definite loss of his usual ability to come back quickly."[10]

On February 2, the president underwent minor surgery at the Bethesda Naval Hospital for the removal of a cyst on the back of his head. The incision, which required eight stitches, healed normally. It is unknown whether McIntire, who was in attendance with three other physicians, ordered a biopsy and if so, what the results were.

In his long presidency, Franklin Roosevelt returned to his family estate, Springwood, situated on the east side of the Hudson River about two miles south of the village of Hyde Park, New York, as often as his schedule permitted. This comfortable red-clapboard home of seventeen rooms was the place of Roosevelt's birth and the place he loved most. During the first three months of 1944, he spent over two weeks there during three separate trips. His distant cousin, Margaret Suckley, who was secretly in love with him, lived nearby at her family home, a turreted five-story Queen Anne mansion with thirty-five rooms, called Wilderstein. She was then employed at the FDR Library. They saw one another frequently. Margaret kept a diary that was not discovered by historians until after her death in 1991, in her one-hundredth year. Her diary guardedly revealed her concerns about him:

Jan. 22nd Saturday: I went out into the warm sunshine to greet him. He looks better than I expected, but says he still gets tired very easily...[11]

Feb. 24th Thursday: The P. is tired, as I have said before. He acknowledges it and wants to get out of his grueling job, but there is too much demand for him to stay in, not only from this country, but also from all the United Nations—if one could look into the future![12]

Mar. 27th Monday: I went over to the house at 9, to say good-bye to the P. His fever was down and he had cereal and milk for breakfast and orange juice. He left at 25 minutes of 11. He is prepared to go to the hospital tomorrow and be X-rayed, etc. I pray they do the right thing by him.[13]

If Eleanor Roosevelt had been especially worried about her husband's health that March, she likely would have stayed close to home; however, on March 4, she left Washington for a tour of military installations in the Caribbean and South America from which she did not return until March 28. All of her life Eleanor Roosevelt was sensitive of those less fortunate than she, but she was strangely oblivious of the possibility that something was dreadfully wrong with her husband.

The one person on the White House staff who was the most solicitous of the president's needs was Grace Tully, a secretary then in her mid-forties. One of her male colleagues affectionately referred to her as "Lady Abbess." Indeed, under other circumstances Grace could have been the esteemed superior of a convent of nuns. Her calling, however, was to serve the president of the United States, for whom she had worked for over a decade with loyalty and devotion.

In March, Grace became extremely concerned about the president's health. She later wrote,

In the last year I found the Boss occasionally nodding over his mail or dozing a moment during dictation. . . . But as it began to occur with increasing frequency I became seriously alarmed. . . . After some troubled thought over the matter I finally decided to talk to Anna about it. She was as deeply concerned as I and, when I went a step further a few days later in speaking to Dr. McIntire, I found that she already had talked it over with him.[14]

Anna Roosevelt Boettiger, the president's only daughter and his eldest child, had become a permanent resident of the White House in February, along with her two children, Buzzie and Sistie, and her husband, John. Anna, then in her late thirties, was attractive and well liked. During her mother's frequent absences from Washington, she acted as unofficial White House hostess. Literally seeing her father failing before her eyes, Anna demanded that McIntire bring in a specialist. Although McIntire resented Anna's intrusion into what he considered his exclusive area of responsibility, he agreed to have her father examined by a cardiologist. On March 28, Lieutenant Commander Howard G. Bruenn, the head of cardiology at the Bethesda Naval Hospital, examined the president for the first time. He was thirty-nine, only slightly older than the president's daughter.

Bruenn was an excellent choice. He had graduated from Johns Hopkins Medical School in 1929, near the top of his class. Following an internship at Boston City Hospital, he had been an assistant resident at Columbia Presbyterian Hospital from 1932 to 1934. During the next two years, he was chief resident at Columbia Presbyterian, where he worked closely with Dr. Robert Levy, one of the outstanding cardiologists of his day. Before World War II, he had practiced cardiology on his own. When the war came, he volunteered for the Navy. In March 1944, he was Chief of Cardiology at the Bethesda Naval Hospital.

Bruenn would never forget Tuesday, March 28, 1944, the day on which he first examined the president. He was immediately struck by the president's poor appearance. Roosevelt's face was gray and he appeared to be very tired. Bruenn recalled long afterward that he suspected something was terribly wrong as soon as he saw him. What was terribly wrong was the president's enlarged heart. It could no longer pump sufficient quantities of blood to meet his body's requirements for oxygen and nutrients.

Without giving his patient any information about his truly awful condition, Bruenn promptly conveyed his findings and their interpretation to Admiral McIntire. These findings included hypertension, hypertensive heart disease, cardiac failure (left ventricular), and acute bronchitis. Except for the bronchitis, these problems had been completely unsuspected by McIntire.

Admiral McIntire reacted to Bruenn's diagnosis with a flurry of activity. He ordered Bruenn to keep quiet about his findings and to refrain from giving the president any information except in response to a direct question. He ordered an immediate consultation with a group of senior Navy doctors including Captain John Harper, Commanding Officer, Bethesda Naval Hospital, Captain Robert Duncan, executive officer of the Bethesda Naval Hospital and Captain Charles Behrens, officer in command, radiology department of the Bethesda Naval Hospital. He urgently requested two honorary consultants of the Navy, Dr. James A. Paullin, president of the AMA, and Dr. Frank H. Lahey, head of the Lahey Clinic in Boston, to drop everything and to come to Bethesda as soon as possible. In addition, he directed Bruenn to prepare a memorandum of recommendations for treatment of the president's condition.

If Lieutenant Commander Bruenn was the slightest bit nervous at becoming the focus of all this attention, he never showed it. He produced a list of recommendations. These included total bed rest for one to two weeks, digitalization of .4g of digitalis daily for five days, subsequently .1g every day, reduction of salt intake, codeine for control of cough, sedation to ensure a good night's sleep, and gradual weight reduction. McIntire made short shrift of these recommendations in their entirety, telling Bruenn, "You can't do that. This is the President of the United States!"[15]

On the afternoon of March 31, Drs. Paullin and Lahey, who had already studied the president's history and test results, examined him for the first time. Afterward they had extensive discussions with McIntire and Bruenn. For unknown reasons, Dr. Lahey seemed primarily interested in the president's gastrointestinal tract. He indicated that while no surgical procedure was indicated, the situation was serious enough to warrant fully apprising the president of his condition. Dr. Paullin agreed with Bruenn's diagnosis of congestive heart failure, but was not persuaded that the condition was serious enough to require digitalization. Bruenn stood his ground and soon convinced Paullin to drop his opposition to that drug.

McIntire partially reversed himself, tacitly approving most of the treatment that Bruenn had outlined and informing him, "if you have rapport with the president, this is now your problem."[16] Lahey's recommendation that the president be fully informed was quietly ignored. Bruenn would always remember, "He never asked me a question about the medications I was giving him, what his blood pressure was, nothing. He was not interested."[17]

The president received his initial dose of digitalis in the amount of .5g on March 31. After some time the doctors were able to get him to reduce his tobacco consumption to six cigarettes a day. Although complete bed rest had been ruled out, the president was encouraged to leave Washington for an extended vacation. Neither Franklin Roosevelt nor any member of his family was told the hard truth that congestive heart failure was often fatal.

Roosevelt eagerly embraced the idea of a change to a warmer climate far removed from the corridors of power. When his longtime friend, Bernard Baruch, offered his South Carolina plantation, Hobcaw, FDR gladly accepted. Baruch, a native South Carolinian, who had made a fortune as a young man in New York City, owned one of the great plantations in his native state. It was situated on the Waccamaw River about ten miles from the sea and measured 16,000 acres of fields and woods. Like so many others, Baruch assumed that all the president needed was a good rest. He later wrote: "There are few better places to rest than Hobcaw. It has no annoying distractions of any kind, not even a telephone. The big brick house, situated on a knoll overlooking the Waccamaw River, is surrounded by a broad expanse of fields, woods and streams. The gardens would be in bloom when the President was there, and then it would be one of the loveliest places on earth."[18]

Before departing for the South, Roosevelt arranged for a private meeting with an experienced political correspondent for the *New York Times,* Turner Catledge, who had just completed a trip around the country to ascertain the president's prospects. When Catledge was summoned to the White House in early April, he had not seen the president for over four months. He would never forget their meeting:

> When I entered the President's office, and had my first glimpse of him in several months, I was shocked and horrified—so much so that my impulse was to turn around and leave. I felt I was seeing something I shouldn't see. He had lost a great deal of weight. His shirt collar hung so loose on his neck that you could have put your hand inside it. He was sitting there with a vague, glassy-eyed expression on his face and his mouth hanging open.
>
> Reluctantly, I sat down and we started talking. I expected him to ask me about the political situation, but he never did. He would start talking about something, then in mid-sentence he would stop and his mouth would drop open and he'd sit staring at me in silence. I knew I was looking at a terribly sick man.[19]

• • •

> . . . and my talk with him lasted more than an hour. His appointments secretary, General Edwin M. (Pa) Watson, came to the door several times but Roosevelt would raise his hand (a hand so thin you could almost see through it) and tell me to stay. I had the impression of a man who very badly wanted someone to talk to. And so we talked on, although he never brought up politics. Repeatedly he would lose his train of thought, stop, and stare blankly at me. It was an agonizing experience for me. Finally a waiter brought his lunch, and Watson said his luncheon guest was waiting, and I was able to make my escape.[20]

Catledge now had an opportunity to do a major story on the president's health, which could have destroyed his chances of being reelected. James (Scotty) Reston, a thirty-four-year-old reporter for the *Times* covering his first presidential election, learned of Catledge's concerns about the president's health. Much later, Reston confirmed that Catledge had decided to keep the story under wraps. The most probable explanation was that their meeting was private and off the record.

The president's train reached Hobcaw on Easter Sunday, April 9. His entourage included Admiral McIntire, Lieutenant Commander Bruenn and Admiral William D. Leahy, his representative on the Joint Chiefs of Staff, who had been a friend from the time Roosevelt was assistant secretary of the Navy in World War I. The president remained at Hobcaw for four weeks, sleeping late every morning and fishing or exploring the countryside in the afternoons.

On April 25, Mrs. Roosevelt flew down to Hobcaw with her daughter, Anna, and the Prime Minister of Australia, John Curtin, and his wife. The First Lady did not linger. On May 1, Margaret Suckley listened to a radio broadcast of Eleanor Roosevelt's press conference. The First Lady told the press that "she had seen the president last week, that he looked very well, but that he might be staying away for another week to complete his cure."[21] Mrs. Roosevelt remained ignorant of her husband's condition.

At the president's urging, Margaret Suckley joined him at Hobcaw on May 4. On her arrival, she was informed that the president had experienced some sort of intestinal attack. It was later diagnosed as gallstones. When they had some time alone, he gave her bits of two letters which he had never gotten around to finishing. They were published with Miss Suckley's diary in 1995. One of the letters reads in part, "I forgot to tell you that Dr. Bruin [*sic*] came down, too—He is one of the best heart men—Tho' my own is definitely better—does queer things still—I wish so you were here."[22]

Miss Suckley soon learned that the president's doctors were withholding certain things from him. On May 5, she wrote,

> After lunch Mr. Baruch and Dr. Bruenn left by plane for Wash. (with the mail pouch). I had a good talk with the P. about himself . . . He said he discovered that the doctors had not agreed together about what to tell him, so that he found out that they were not telling him the whole truth & that he was evidently more sick than they said! It is foolish of them to attempt to put anything over on him![23]

Throughout his lengthy interlude at Hobcaw, Franklin Roosevelt seemed content. He accepted, with his usual composure, the news that he was a sicker man than he had thought. There is no evidence that he ever asked Bruenn to reveal the whole truth. In a letter to Harry Hopkins, he wrote, "I slept twelve hours of the twenty-four, sat in the sun, never lost my temper and decided to let the world go hang. The interesting thing is the world didn't hang."[24]

After his return to the White House on May 7, the president endeavored to follow the reduced work schedule which Bruenn thought essential. The day after his return, he instructed Pa Watson to hold his appointments to a minimum. He informed his staff that he would only accept appointments between 11 A.M. and 1 P.M., that he would avoid all business lunches, that he would rest for an hour and a half after lunch, following which he would sign papers for no more than two hours.

In the late afternoon of May 11, he left Washington for Shangri-La, his retreat in the Catoctin Mountains of Maryland, where he "planned complete relaxation"[25] over a long weekend. Four days later, he boarded the presidential train for Hyde Park, arriving there in time for breakfast on the morning of Friday, May 19. On the trip north, he confided to one of his staff that he was determined to sleep twelve hours every night. He spent six nights at his Hudson Valley estate. In April and May the president had spent almost six weeks away from the White House at Hobcaw, Shangri-la and Hyde Park.

On June 8, at a press and radio conference, Admiral McIntire briefed reporters on the president's health. The *New York Times* carried the story the next day under Charles Hurd's byline with a headline that proclaimed, "President's Health

'Excellent,' Admiral McIntire Reports." McIntire fielded the reporters' questions as follows:

> Reporter: Ross, just to get a definitive statement here, what do you think of the president's present health, now?
>
> McIntire: His present health is excellent, I can say that—.
>
> Reporter: In all respects?
>
> McIntire: In all respects when I say excellent, you can't go much more than that.
>
> • • •
>
> Reporter: He is in better physical shape than the average man of his age?
>
> McIntire: Better physical condition.
>
> Reporter: For the record, Ross, can we have what was wrong with him? He had sinus, bronchitis and the intestinal upset—
>
> McIntire: (interposing) He had his influenza. That was the start of the whole thing. There were complications following influenza.
>
> Reporter: What are "these" now?
>
> McIntire: He had the intestinal upset, then he picked up this acute cold, which was followed with his sinus infection and his acute bronchitis.
>
> • • •
>
> Reporter: Ross, there was a very prevalent rumor around here that bronchitis was bronchial pneumonia?
>
> McIntire: No, not at all.
>
> Reporter: Also a rumor that there was quite a bit of trouble with his heart, maybe?
>
> McIntire: No. I have been very factual with you. I have given the exact—
>
> Steve Early: (interposing) I don't think it is a good thing to start denying rumors.[26]

Early, Roosevelt's longtime press secretary, was almost certainly trying to avoid any more questions about the president's heart. His stratagem succeeded. There were no follow-up questions about any heart problem. McIntire's statements that day were unique. No other medical authority had ever told the American people more flagrant lies about the health of their president.

McIntire's famous patient invariably read the *New York Times* in bed every morning with his breakfast tray. He would have seen Charles Hurd's story and would have known that the admiral had pulled the wool over the public's eyes, to which FDR, being the politician that he was, would not have objected. Still, he had ample reason for being dissatisfied with his personal physician. McIntire had failed to diagnose his congestive heart failure. He had failed to have the president examined by a competent heart specialist until the president's daughter had insisted. Furthermore, McIntire had concealed the full truth from the president about his heart condition, for which there was no cure. One has to question Roosevelt's judgment in not replacing McIntire before making the fateful decision to seek a fourth term. Apparently, Franklin Roosevelt sought no medical advice on whether he should run again except from his old friend, who had been his physician for over ten years. After the president's death, McIntire wrote, "With proper care and strict adherence to rules, I gave it my best judgment that his chances of winning through to 1948 were *good*."[27]

The president announced his decision to run for a fourth term on July 11, less than a week before the Democratic Convention in Chicago. On July 19, Roosevelt arrived by train in San Diego en route to Hawaii for a meeting with General Douglas MacArthur and Admiral Chester W. Nimitz. His party included both McIntire and Bruenn. His eldest son, Lieutenant Colonel James Roosevelt, U.S. Marine Corps, was then on temporary duty as an intelligence officer at nearby Camp Pendleton. Early the next morning, James joined his father on the presidential railroad car, the Ferdinand Magellan. The president's schedule that day was formidable. In the morning he was to observe an amphibious exercise involving 10,000 marines of the Fifth Marine Division who were about to be sent into combat. That same day the Democratic Convention in Chicago would nominate him as the party's candidate. The uncertainty over whom the party would nominate for vice president still weighed on the president. He was to make his acceptance speech that evening from the Ferdinand Magellan over a radio hookup that would be broadcast live to the delegates in Chicago.

Shortly before he was to leave for the Marine landing exercise, the president turned white and gasped that he was having horrible abdominal pains. He and James decided not to summon his physicians. James managed to help his father from his berth onto the floor where he lay for perhaps ten minutes, experiencing spasms of pain. Some years later, James wrote that "Father lay on the floor of the railroad car, his eyes closed, his face drawn, his powerful torso occasionally convulsed as the waves of pain stabbed him. Never in all my life had I felt so alone with him—and so helpless."[28]

The president knew what he had to do. To cancel his schedule, much less his speech, was unthinkable. He made himself carry on as if nothing had happened. This entire episode was carefully concealed from everyone including McIntire; however, one photograph on that day focused attention on the president's health. This was taken during his rereading of selected portions of his acceptance speech for photographers and movie cameramen. It showed the president looking glassy eyed, with his mouth open. When this photograph was published in numerous newspapers, Steve Early, FDR's press secretary, was furious. The hapless photographer who had caught FDR in the act of speaking was kicked off the tour.

In Hawaii, the president was faced with conflicting advice concerning the next major offensive against the Japanese Empire. Admiral Ernest J. King, the Commander in Chief of the U.S. Navy, and the Chief of Naval Operations, who had been in Hawaii a few days ahead of the president, had made it clear to Admiral Nimitz, commander of U.S. Naval forces in the Pacific, that he wanted to bypass the Philippines in favor of a full-scale invasion of Formosa (now known as Taiwan). King's plan was anathema to General MacArthur, who was determined to liberate the Philippines. According to King's sources, MacArthur had asked President Roosevelt "if he were willing to accept responsibility for breaking a solemn promise to 18,000,000 Christian Filipinos that the Americans would return."[29] King concluded that "in the end this argument carried the day."[30] The president subsequently ordered the Joint Chiefs to adopt MacArthur's strategic plan.

Of their private conversation, MacArthur wrote, "We talked of everything but the war—of our old carefree days when life was simpler and gentler, of many things that had disappeared in the mists of time."[31] MacArthur found the decline in the president's physical condition all too obvious. "I had not seen him for a number of years, and physically he was just a shell of the man I had known. It was clearly evident that his days were numbered."[32]

The president's Pacific voyage ended at the Bremerton Navy Yard in Washington State. On the afternoon of August 12, several thousand soldiers and civilians crowded around both sides of a dry dock to hear the president speak from the bridge of the destroyer *Cummings*. Admiral McIntire and Lieutenant Commander Bruenn were standing nearby. While he was speaking, the president experienced severe pain in his chest that radiated into his shoulders. Bruenn remembered what happened after the speech:

> He kept on with the speech and came below and said "I had a severe pain!" We stripped him down in the cabin of the ship, took a cardiogram, some blood and so forth, and fortunately it was a transient episode, a so-called angina, not a myocardial infarction. But that was really a very disturbing situation . . . This was proof positive that he had coronary disease, no question about it." [33]

In far-off Wilderstein, Margaret Suckley suspecting something was wrong wrote, "It seemed to me as though he was tired and that he once or twice got mixed up on his words . . . any tiny slip of any kind always worries me! I hope I am all wrong and that he is feeling wonderfully rested & benefited by the trip."[34]

Roosevelt returned to Washington on August 17, after being away from the White House for thirty-five days. The next day he was photographed on the west lawn of the White House under a magnolia tree planted by Andrew Jackson, having lunch with Harry Truman, his recently nominated running mate. One of the photographers was twenty-eight-year-old George Tames, son of Greek immigrants, who had worked his way up from poverty to become an assistant White House photographer. Tames idolized Roosevelt, but he was not blind to reality. Late in his life he wrote, "By the time I was one of this small group of photographers, there was no question in my mind that President Roosevelt was dying."[35] Tames' photograph of the president and the future president has survived. The contrast between them is striking. Truman, who was sixty, looked younger. Roosevelt was sixty-two, but he appeared ten years older. Afterward, Truman told a friend that the president's hands were shaking so badly that he could barely pour cream in his coffee.

In 1944, the only formal conference between Roosevelt and Churchill took place in Quebec in September. They had not seen each other since December 1943, when they had met in Cairo after the Teheran Conference. At Quebec, Churchill became so concerned about the changes he saw in Roosevelt that he took the liberty of asking Admiral McIntire for a confidential statement about the president's health. By then McIntire was hopelessly entangled in a web of his own deceit. McIntire later recalled, "I gave (Churchill) the results of our June checkup, proving that there was nothing organically wrong, but not hesitating to stress the president's age (62) and the fact that for twelve years he had been under constant strain. If . . . he does not overdo there is every reason to believe that he can win through."[36] Churchill was not entirely reassured. Lord Moran, Churchill's personal physician, had accompanied the prime minister to Quebec. His private thoughts would have shocked the American public.

> For my part, I wondered how far Roosevelt's health impaired his judgment and sapped his resolve to get to the bottom of each problem before it came up for discussion. At Quebec he seemed to me to have but a couple of stone in weight—you could have put your fist between his neck and his collar—and I said to myself then that men at this time of life do not go thin all of a sudden just for nothing.[37]

Throughout the Quebec Conference and the subsequent visit that Churchill made to Hyde Park, Roosevelt stayed reasonably well except for one surge in his blood pressure while he and Churchill watched a film that vividly depicted Woodrow Wilson's cruel, final illness.

The president's reelection campaign was carefully crafted to protect him from overdoing himself. By the standards of any recent presidential campaign, it was almost a leisurely affair. There were no airplane trips. All travel between cities was done in the comfort of the president's train. There were only four major addresses outside Washington, all of which were on the East Coast except for one in Chicago. This last hurrah turned out to be a tonic for Franklin Roosevelt. Not only did he look better, he clearly enjoyed campaigning against his younger opponent, forty-two-year-old Thomas E. Dewey. In the middle of his presidential campaign, Roosevelt summoned Turner Catledge to the White House. The journalist later wrote:

> So I started for the White House, but with an unhappy, squeamish feeling, remembering how it had been the last time I had seen him. But when I walked into his office, a new man was sitting there beaming at me. He was still thin and emaciated but

he had life and spirit in his face, and I remember thinking. "It's the campaign that revived him—politics is this man's life's blood" [38]

The president's apparent physical comeback was not always discernible. Joseph P. Kennedy, former ambassador to the Court of St. James's, met with Roosevelt early in the afternoon on Thursday, October 26, at the president's request. Kennedy had not been eager to see him. Four years earlier, the president had terminated Kennedy's governmental service by recalling him from London. Kennedy, who was then fifty-two, would remain bitter for the rest of his life over Roosevelt's failure to give him another assignment. That Thursday, the president received Kennedy at the White House in the hope of gaining his public endorsement. It never materialized. After what would be their last meeting, Kennedy recorded his impressions of the president's health:

> If I hadn't been warned by the stories of his illness and the fact that Archbishop Spellman told me he looked very badly, I would have been shocked beyond words. He sat behind his desk and his face was as gray as his hair, put out his hand in a very friendly manner, and asked me to sit down. During the entire conversation, I was convinced that he was far from a well man. He is thin; he has an unhealthy color. His hands shake violently when he tries to take a drink of water. About 10 percent of the time that he is talking, his words are not clearly enunciated. [39]

Three days later, Kennedy learned that the candidate for vice president, Harry S. Truman, and the chairman of the Democratic National Committee both felt that President Roosevelt would not live long. In his diary, Kennedy wrote,

> I couldn't help but think if the world knew that the candidate for vice-president and the chairman of the Democratic National Committee were sitting in my room telling me that they hated the crowd that ran things in Washington and wouldn't keep them there five minutes, and that Roosevelt wouldn't live long and they would run things right—no wonder I am not going to do anything. [40]

On November 7, Franklin Roosevelt was re-elected President of the United States for his fourth term. He and Mrs. Roosevelt spent Thanksgiving at Hyde Park. The following Monday, he left Washington by train for Warm Springs. The president had invited Margaret Suckley to join him. Because of her hectic schedule, Mrs. Roosevelt remained in Washington. On the matter of the president's health, Margaret was unusually perceptive. By the end of November, she knew that the benefits of the fall campaign had not lasted. Her diary for November 29 is somber reading:

> I found myself looking at the President at least half the time. He looked pale, thin and tired. I try so hard to make myself think he looks well, but he doesn't . . . He looks ten years older than last year, to me—of course I wouldn't confess that to anyone, least of all to him, but he knows it himself.[41]

The president remained at Warm Springs for almost three weeks. During this time, he was under the care of at least three doctors. Both McIntire and Bruenn had traveled with him on the overnight train trip from Washington, but the admiral only stayed three nights in Warm Springs. Around December 12, Dr. Robert Duncan, a chest specialist and the executive officer of the Bethesda Naval Hospital, arrived in Warm Springs for the ostensible reason of inspecting the polio hospital. The undisclosed reason almost certainly related to the president's heart condition. On December 6, Bruenn had become alarmed when the president's blood pressure shot up after mild exercise in a heated swimming pool and he very likely summoned Dr. Duncan. Margaret Suckley was not fooled by the explanation for Dr. Duncan's presence. On December 14 she wrote:

> The night before last (the president) was dictating to me from the sofa when Dr. Bruenn, Geo. Fox and Dr. Duncan came in about 9:30. Dr. Duncan has come down to look over the polio hospital and, I suspect, primarily to see the Pres. & see how he is getting along . . . I am hoping to get a little closer to the doctors so that they will talk more freely to me. But they put on, or rather keep on, their doctors' manner and tell you nothing. They seem to be concentrating on the Pres.' heart. He himself said it was a "cardiac" condition, and that his muscles are "deteriorating" and that they don't know why.[42]

Although the president had been away from the White House for the better part of a month, he remained in Washington less than a week before departing for Hyde Park two days before Christmas. His devoted secretary, William D. Hassett, who was almost a member of the family, accompanied him. Two months earlier, Hassett had been sanguine about the president's health. On October 21, the president had in one day managed a four-hour ride in an open car during a heavy rain through four of the five boroughs of New York City, an appearance at Ebbets Field, and a major foreign policy speech at the Waldorf-Astoria. He had suffered no apparent harm. Afterward, Hassett had written, "Best of all, my own fears and misgivings about the President's health . . . are dissipated, vanished like the morning dew."[43] On Christmas Day, Hassett accepted an invitation to have dinner with the Roosevelts. The diffident Hassett quietly watched the president at the head of the table beneath the Delano portraits. That night he confided to his diary, "I fear for his health despite assurances from the doctors that he is O.K."[44]

The president boarded his train on Friday night, December 29, at Highland, across the river from Hyde Park, for Washington. As the train rolled southward through the silent, snow-covered countryside, the president could look back on 1944 with both satisfaction and concern. He had been reelected president for an unprecedented fourth term; yet he must have known that his health was failing and that the odds of surviving another four years were long. They were a lot longer than he or anyone knew. The president's life was ebbing away. At the end of the year, he had less than three-and-a-half months to live.

CHAPTER THREE

The Selection of Truman

*"We called the President, who was on his private car en route
to the Pacific Coast, and I insisted that he again tell these men that
he wished Truman for a running mate."*

EDWARD J. FLYNN

CHAIRMAN OF THE DEMOCRATIC EXECUTIVE COMMITTEE OF
BRONX COUNTY, ALSO KNOWN AS THE BOSS OF THE BRONX.

One week before Harry S. Truman was nominated to be the Democratic candidate for vice president, President Roosevelt told James F. Byrnes of South Carolina, the former Senator and Supreme Court Justice, and then head of the Office of War Mobilization, that he barely knew Truman, who had been a Senator from Missouri since 1935. It is hardly surprising that they had not become close. Their backgrounds could not have been more different. Roosevelt came from the landed gentry of the Hudson River Valley. He bore a famous name. He was a graduate of Groton and Harvard. Most of his adult life had involved elective offices. Before being elected president, he had been a New York state senator, assistant secretary of the Navy and governor of New York. He had never had to struggle to earn a living.

Harry S. Truman never had the opportunity to attend either a famous prepara-
tory school or a renowned university. He never went to college. Before World War
I, he did hard manual labor on a farm, often working from sunup to sundown.
When the United States declared war on Germany in 1917, he volunteered for the
Missouri National Guard at the age of thirty-three. In France, he earned the rank of
captain and the command of Battery D, part of the 2nd battalion, 129th Field
Artillery. He never went back to the farm. After his discharge, Truman and an army
buddy, Eddie Jacobson, opened a men's clothing store located at 104 West 12th
Street, Kansas City, on the ground floor of the Glennon Hotel. In 1922 their busi-
ness failed. Two years before, thirty-eight-year-old Franklin Roosevelt was nominated to run for vice president of the United States on the Democratic ticket with
Governor James Cox of Ohio. Many political observers already considered young
Roosevelt a future president. No one would have considered Harry Truman a future
senator, much less a future president.

Harry Truman's first elective office was as Judge of Jackson County, Missouri,
an administrative position equivalent to a county commissioner. He took his oath
of office on New Year's Day, 1923. Just over a decade passed before Truman had his
chance to make the quantum leap from the County Court House to the United
States capitol. To his astonishment, he was selected by T. J. Pendergast, the boss of
the most powerful political machine in the state, to run for the Senate. With the
financial and organizational support of the Pendergast machine, Truman defeated
two other candidates in the Democratic primary and went on to win the general
election in November 1934.

Six years later, Truman was reelected to the Senate after narrowly defeating the
then governor of Missouri, Lloyd C. Stark, in the primary. A loss in the primary likely would have ended Truman's political career. His win was due in no small part to
an ambitious, young politician named Robert E. Hannegan, who was a powerhouse
in St. Louis politics. Late in that primary race, Hannegan switched sides. He dis-
avowed Governor Stark and ordered his ward heelers and precinct bosses to support
Truman, who defeated Stark by only 8,000 votes out of 665,000 cast.

In early 1944, Henry A. Wallace seemed to be Roosevelt's choice for vice president. Wallace came from a prominent Iowa family of agronomists, and was considered an expert on hybridizing corn. He had served as secretary of agriculture from
March 1933 through 1940. At the 1940 Democratic Convention, Roosevelt had

forced a reluctant convention to accept Wallace as his running mate. Over the next four years, Vice President Wallace had accumulated some formidable enemies. He was disliked by Southerners because of his outspoken opposition to racial segregation. Conservatives suspected him of being prone to communistic ideas. The big city bosses resented him because he was too independent. In spite of his detractors, a Gallup poll taken in early March 1944, showed that Wallace was the first choice for vice president among 46 percent of rank-and-file Democrats. Cordell Hull, the secretary of state, was far behind with 21 percent and former Postmaster James A. Farley was in third place with 13 percent. The rank and file of organized labor were among Wallace's strongest supporters. Indeed, the single most important labor leader in the country had pledged his support. This was Sidney Hillman, president of the Amalgamated Clothing Workers of America and former vice president of the CIO. Hillman was the driving force behind the CIO's new Political Action Committee, which for the first time was venturing into a presidential election. Wallace's political future, however, would depend neither on polls nor on organized labor. His fate would be decided by one man, the president of the United States.

After a Cabinet meeting on March 3, Wallace met privately with FDR. At one point, Wallace broached the possibility of a mission to Russia in the near future. The president replied, "I think they are going to be shooting at you during the campaign for being too far to the left. My own feeling is that you had better not go to Russia."[1] FDR's constraint on his travels because of political considerations seemed to reassure Wallace that they were still a team.

Apart from the president, the power structure in the Democratic Party included three main groups. There were the labor unions led by Hillman's Political Action Committee. There were the congressional leaders including Alben W. Barkley, Scott Lucus, Millard Tydings, and Harry Byrd in the Senate and Sam Rayburn in the House. Last, there were the big city bosses. Of these, Frank Hague of New Jersey, who held absolute power in Jersey City and Hudson County, was the most notorious. In 1944, he was a member of the Democratic National Committee and a delegate to the Democratic Convention. He was less influential in national politics than Edward J. Kelly, the mayor of Chicago, and Edward J. Flynn, of New York, known as the boss of the Bronx, who were far closer to FDR

Kelly had become mayor of Chicago in 1933 after the death of Mayor Anton J. Cermak who on February 15, 1933, was mortally wounded in Miami by a would-be assassin of President-elect Roosevelt. Kelly's biographer, Roger Biles, has written of him,

> For fourteen crucial years, spanning the Great Depression and Second World War, Edward J. Kelly ruled Chicago's city hall and its Democratic party. . . . Kelly's enterprising strategy involved several elements: attracting traditionally Republican black voters to the Democratic fold, allying the machine with President Franklin D. Roosevelt's New Deal, and tapping the financial resources of organized crime.[2]

For a brief period in 1939, it appeared that the attorney general of the United States, Frank Murphy, was on a collision course with Mayor Kelly. Secretary of the Interior Harold L. Ickes was well aware of the corruption that permeated Chicago, which was his hometown. In December 1939, he learned that the attorney general planned to seek federal grand jury indictments against prominent Chicago politicians. Ickes' secret diary, which was not published until 1954, revealed the high hurdle that Murphy faced.

> Frank then said he wanted very much to clean up Chicago because he thought that it was the worst mess in the country and that he hoped "they" would let him go ahead. I found out that it was surmised that the President would not permit Murphy to go ahead with this investigation on account of Ed Kelly. This I consider unfortunate because Chicago so badly needs a thorough renovating. Murphy told me that the Department of Justice had all the goods that it needed on the Chicago crooks and apparently he is only waiting for the green light which probably will not flash.[3]

Neither Murphy nor the two attorneys general who followed him, Robert H. Jackson and Francis Biddle, were ever given the green light to clean up Chicago. When the death of Justice Butler on November 16, 1939, created a vacancy on the Supreme Court, the president sent to the Senate the nomination of Frank Murphy as associate justice of the Supreme Court. Murphy's biographer, Sidney Fine, has speculated, "it may be, however, that Roosevelt wished to rid himself of an attorney general whose successful prosecution of city bosses and threatened prosecution of others posed a threat to the president's third term ambitions."[4]

The boss of the Bronx, Edward J. Flynn, had more influence on FDR for a longer period of time on purely political matters than anyone else with the possible exception of Louis Howe, who had died in 1936. In 1940, Roosevelt had arranged for Flynn to become chairman of the Democratic National Committee. This appointment did not sit well with Ickes, who wrote in his diary:

> For whatever reason the appointment was made, in my judgment it was an unfortunate one. Flynn is a typical big-city political boss in alliance with Tammany Hall. To be sure, he broke with Tammany in 1932 to support the president, but I believe that there has been a *rapprochement* since. In any event, Flynn is what he is—a man who has become rich out of politics and who has enriched his friends, while building up what is acknowledged to be a very powerful machine in the Bronx.[5]

On February 12, 1943, Vice President Wallace had a painful conversation with Flynn that revealed his blatant anti-Semitism:

> Flynn is very much prejudiced against the Jews and urged me to read a book by Hilaire Belloc about the Jews. He [Flynn] bemoaned the fact that the Jews had control of all phases of the amusement business, movies, radio, song writers, theater, etc. He said the trouble with their having control is that in this way they consciously or unconsciously impose on all the people in the United States, their own ideals of what culture really is. I said I hadn't noticed this in the movies. He said he could name a hundred movies portraying the sufferings of the downtrodden Jews. I challenged him to name one and he couldn't. Ed likes to pose as a man of very great culture . . . Ed says that the Bronx is 60 percent Jewish but every time a Jew sticks up his head in the Bronx he knocks it down.[6]

Early in the war, Roosevelt had considered appointing Flynn ambassador to China, then perhaps the most difficult diplomatic assignment in the world. James F. Byrnes gave this account of a conversation with the president about Flynn's qualifications. "Sometime afterward, when I was in Mr. Roosevelt's office he had asked me how I thought the Senate would react should he name Flynn Ambassador to China. My reply was in the form of a question: 'What qualifications does he have for that particular assignment?' The President said, 'None. But he wants it, and I am anxious to do something for him.'"[7] Roosevelt quietly dropped the idea.

In January 1943 Flynn resigned as chairman of the Democratic National Committee in hopes of becoming the new minister to Australia. On January 8, Roosevelt wrote him, "I am sending your nomination to the Senate on Monday as Minister to Australia. In addition I am appointing you my personal representative with the rank of Ambassador. I do so because in the very large area of the Southwest Pacific, I want to feel free to avail myself of your services in various forms of activity, over and above your duties as Minister."[8] Byrnes recalled, "when that appointment went to the Senate in January, 1943, there was a storm of objection."[9] Facing certain defeat in the Senate, Flynn was encouraged by Byrnes and Senate Majority Leader Barkley to withdraw his name. Flynn finally did so the day before the Senate was scheduled to vote on his confirmation. At Flynn's request, Byrnes had suggested the wording of his letter of withdrawal. At the time, Flynn did not seem to resent Byrnes' role; however, a year later Byrnes would have occasion to wonder.

In January 1944, Robert E. Hannegan, then forty, became chairman of the Democratic National Committee. Ed Flynn later described his role in Hannegan's appointment:

> In the later part of 1943, when I was in Florida, Mayor Edward J. Kelly of Chicago came to visit me. We discussed at length the question of a successor to Walker as National Chairman. Kelly suggested the name of Robert Hannegan, the Commissioner of Internal Revenue. Mayor Kelly did not know Hannegan personally, but knew of his good reputation. He felt that Bob would be a good chairman. I agreed with him. I had become acquainted with Hannegan when he was a candidate for the position of Internal Revenue Collector for the district of St. Louis, Missouri. Later I met him in connection with my work in the National Committee. When Guy T. Helvering retired from the office of Commissioner of Internal Revenue, I recommended Hannegan to the President as a successor, entirely because of the fine record he had made in Missouri. When I returned from Florida, I spoke to the President about Hannegan as a suitable man for the Chairmanship of the National Committee. After some consideration Roosevelt agreed, and the National Committee elected Hannegan in January 1944.[10]

Senator Truman was not disappointed by Hannegan's appointment. On January 22, Wallace wrote in his diary, "Senator Truman came in to say he will probably be in St. Louis with me on February 13. He is anxious to have me come to meet Bob Hannegan, the new Chairman of the National Democratic Committee, at a party which the Missouri people are putting on in the Mayflower tonight. Truman repeated what he said, that he was eager to support me for vice-president again, that he and I had seen things just alike, etc., etc. . . . ."[11]

Early in 1944, the new chairman of the Democratic National Committee started compiling a list of the potential vice presidential candidates. It is safe to assume that the name of the junior senator from Missouri was high on his list.

Throughout the winter and spring, Roosevelt kept his own counsel about his political plans. Although the president seldom confided his innermost thoughts to anyone, he was more open with Admiral William D. Leahy than with most. They had become fast friends during World War I when Leahy commanded the secretary of the Navy's dispatch boat, the *Dolphin*, and Roosevelt was assistant secretary of the Navy. After he became president, Roosevelt repeatedly showed his trust and confidence in Leahy. In 1937, he named him chief of Naval Operations. After Leahy retired from active duty with the Navy, the president appointed him governor of Puerto Rico. When the French withdrew from the war in June 1940, the United States continued to maintain diplomatic relations with the government of France, which relocated to the provincial town of Vichy. President Roosevelt selected Admiral Leahy to be the ambassador to Vichy. In July 1942, Roosevelt recalled Leahy to active duty as a four-star admiral and named him his chief of staff. He quickly became the president's closest military advisor, with an office in the White House. He also relied on Leahy for many routine matters. In May 1944, he had requested Leahy to arrange for an inspection cruise to Hawaii and Alaska in July. During their discussion, Leahy "brought up the matter of its bearing on the approaching political campaign. The president replied with much feeling, 'Bill, I just hate to run for election. Perhaps the war will by that time have progressed to a point that will make it unnecessary for me to be a candidate.'"[12]

In late May, Roosevelt had arranged to spend five nights at his family home at Hyde Park. On May 22, Margaret Suckley joined him for afternoon tea. In the privacy of Hilltop Cottage, she raised a question that few had been willing to ask.

I asked him if he had decided on a vice-president. He said: "I haven't even decided if I will run myself." What is going to decide you? For you are practically nominated already. "What will decide me, will be the way I feel in a couple of months. If I know I am not going to be able to carry on for another four years, it wouldn't be fair to the American people to run for another term." But who else is there? "I *have* a candidate but don't breathe it to a soul—there is a man, not a politician, who, [*sic*] I think, I could persuade the country to elect. There would be such a gasp when his name was suggested, that I believe he would have a good chance if he were sold to the Country in the right way!" I did gasp a little when he mentioned the name of Henry J. Kaiser.[13]

At a press conference on Tuesday morning, July 11, Roosevelt finally announced from the White House that he was willing to accept his party's nomination. That evening FDR met with his top political advisors in the blue oval study on the second floor of the White House. In addition to Bob Hannegan, Ed Flynn and Ed Kelly the gathering included Frank Walker, the postmaster general and former chairman of the Democratic National Committee; Edwin W. Pauley, a wealthy California oil executive and treasurer of the Democratic National Committee; George E. Allen, the secretary of the Democratic National Committee, who would later write a gossipy book, *Presidents Who Have Known Me;* and the president's son-in-law, John Boettiger, who arrived late. On that warm, humid summer evening, they took off their jackets and relaxed over drinks in the smoke-filled room. The president strangely had little to say. The unspoken assumption of everyone, except for FDR, was that whoever they chose for vice president would be the next president of the United States. Throughout the evening, Hannegan, Kelly and Flynn leaned toward Senator Harry S. Truman. Unknown to Roosevelt, they had agreed on Truman in advance.

The president indicated concern over Truman's age. He was not sure but he thought Truman was nearly sixty. Someone left the oval study to get the Congressional Directory and, so the story goes, when it arrived, Ed Pauley quietly set it aside, after which the conversation drifted to other matters. Flynn later would write, "the question of Senator Truman's association with the Pendergast machine was thoroughly discussed."[14] Flynn and Hannegan urged Roosevelt to reject the other candidates. They had already convinced FDR that Wallace would hurt the president's chances at reelection. Consequently, they spent little time discussing Wallace. James F. Byrnes was discussed at some length. Most of what FDR heard about Byrnes was negative. As director of Economic Stabilization, Byrnes had persuaded the president to sign a comprehensive executive order, which came to be known as the "Hold-the-Line Order." Byrnes later wrote, "It drastically affected the special interests of many. For example, workers were now prohibited from changing their jobs for higher paying jobs unless the war effort was aided thereby."[15] Some labor leaders perceived this order as anti-labor and held it against Byrnes. A bigger problem was that he came from South Carolina, which along with the rest of the South, was a segregated society. Flynn argued that this factor alone would cost the president the Negro vote in New York. Finally, there was the matter of Byrnes joining the Episcopal Church. He had formerly been a Roman Catholic. Flynn thought this might hurt Byrnes in states with large Catholic populations.

The president brought up William O. Douglas, the forty-six-year-old Supreme Court Justice from Washington State. Roosevelt told the others that he was a good liberal with a boy scout type of quality, and besides that he played an interesting game of poker. None of the others showed the slightest interest in Douglas.

Just before the meeting ended, the tired president turned to Hannegan and said, "Bob, I think you and everyone else here want Truman."[16] As the group headed downstairs, Hannegan returned to speak to Roosevelt. Within a few minutes, he rejoined the others with a handwritten note on which Roosevelt had scrawled, "Bob, I think Truman is the right man, FDR"[17] The next day FDR had second thoughts. Within forty-eight hours, he sent Hannegan a letter on White House stationery which stated that he would be glad to run with either William O. Douglas or Harry S. Truman.

On Thursday, the president compounded the confusion over the vice presidency at a meeting with Henry Wallace, who badly wanted another term as vice president as a spring-board to the presidency. Wallace persuaded Roosevelt to write an endorsement letter of sorts to the permanent chairman of the convention. The next day Roosevelt wrote Senator Samuel D. Johnson of Indiana as follows:

> I have been associated with Henry Wallace during his past four years as Vice President, for eight years earlier while he was Secretary of Agriculture and well before that. I like him and respect him and he is my personal friend. For those

reasons, I personally would vote for his renomination if I were a delegate to the Convention. At the same time, I do not wish to appear in any way as dictating to the Convention. Obviously the Convention must do the deciding . . ."[18]

If Wallace had misconstrued the president's letter, he had not misconstrued Bob Hannegan's behind-the-scene maneuvers. Earlier that week he wrote, "The Hannegan game is to knock me at every possible turn in the hope that Truman will be the ultimate beneficiary."[19]

Back home in Missouri, Truman was unconvinced that he was the president's choice. On July 13, he wrote his wife from a hotel in Kansas City, before departing for Chicago, "Dear Bess: Just gave Mr. Roberts [editor of *The Kansas City Star*] a tough interview saying I didn't want the Vice Presidency . . . Also told the West Virginia and Oklahoma delegations to go for Barkley . . . Mr. Roberts says I have it in the bag if I don't say no—and I've said it as tough as I can."[20]

The president arrived at Hyde Park on Friday morning, July 14, in time for breakfast. In the early afternoon, Roosevelt took a call from Jimmy Byrnes. Byrnes felt that he had a reasonably good chance to get on the ticket because the president had promised him that he would not show any preference in the coming contest. A few hours earlier, Robert E. Hannegan and Frank Walker, the postmaster general, had unsuccessfully tried to convince him that the president favored Truman or Douglas. Byrnes intended to find out for himself. Byrnes, who had been a court reporter as a young man, made a verbatim transcript of their conversation. The following exchange occurred:

> Byrnes: Bob Hannegan and Frank Walker stated today that if at the convention they were asked about your views, they would be obliged to say to their friends that from your statements they concluded you did not prefer Wallace but did prefer Truman first and Douglas second, and that either would be preferable to me because they would cost the ticket fewer votes than I would.
>
> The President: Jimmy, that is all wrong. That is not what I told them. It is what they told me. When we all went over the list I did not say that I preferred anybody or that anybody would cost me votes, but they all agreed that Truman would cost fewer votes than anybody and probably Douglas second. This was the agreement they reached and I had nothing to do with it. I was asking

questions. I did not express myself. Objection to you came from labor people, both Federation and C.I.O.

• • •

Byrnes: If they [Hannegan and Walker] make the statement, notwithstanding your letter to Wallace, that you have expressed a preference for Truman and Douglas, it would make it very difficult for me.

The President: We have to be damned careful about language. They asked if I would object to Truman and Douglas and I said no. That is different from using the word "prefer." That is not expressing a preference because you know I told you I would have no preference.[21]

At the end of the tense conversation, Roosevelt asked Byrnes whether he would "go on and run."[22] Byrnes replied that he was still considering it.

Margaret Suckley worked at the Roosevelt Library most of that day. She was elated that the president might spare a few hours for her. That morning, Anna Boettiger dropped by to tell her that the president was still inclined to let the convention make the choice. The president found time for Margaret late in the afternoon. As was their habit, they headed to Hilltop Cottage for afternoon tea. The president gave Margaret his perspective on the vice-presidency.

Wallace and Byrnes both want the V.P. post. One of them will probably get it. The P. says Wallace is much nearer to the P's thoughts and view of things but is a poor administrator—Byrnes would be a good executive, but (1) he used to be a Catholic, (2) he would lose Negro votes, (3) he would alienate some of labor . . . Both are good old friends of the Pres.[23]

The president's failure to mention either Douglas or Truman is curious. Perhaps he simply did not give either of them a chance of getting the nomination. FDR still had not spoken a single word to Truman about the vice presidency.

At 6:30 that night, the president's train pulled out of the Highland station heading west for San Diego. From there the president planned to proceed by warship to Hawaii for a conference with Admiral Nimitz and General MacArthur.

As with all of his wartime travels, his itinerary was kept secret. The president's entourage included Admiral Leahy, his representative on the Joint Chiefs of Staff; Judge Samuel I. Rosenman, his veteran speech writer; and Grace Tully, his invaluable personal secretary. Since the Democrats were holding their national convention in Chicago the following week, none of them could have been surprised by an unscheduled stop in the Chicago railroad yards. Early Saturday afternoon, Robert Hannegan and Mayor Edward Kelly boarded the train.

After conferring with Roosevelt for an hour, Kelly and Hannegan returned to Kelly's apartment, where Kelly immediately placed a call to Jimmy Byrnes in Washington. He informed Byrnes that, "The President has given us the green light to support you and he wants you in Chicago."[24] Byrnes could not get a confirmation from the president himself, who was temporarily out of touch because he could only make telephone calls from various stops on his way to the West Coast; nevertheless, Byrnes took the next train to Chicago, arriving there on Sunday morning. He was driven in the fire chief's car from the station to Mayor Kelly's apartment where he had breakfast with Kelly and Hannegan. They quoted Roosevelt as saying, "Well, you know Jimmy had been my choice from the very first. Go ahead and name him."[25]

That night Byrnes attended a dinner for party leaders who were converging on Chicago. Hannegan and Kelly told them that Byrnes was Roosevelt's choice. As the meeting was about to break up, Hannegan turned to Kelly and said, "Ed, there is one thing we forgot. The president said, 'Clear it with Sidney.'"[26] They were referring to the labor leader, Sidney Hillman, who was Wallace's most important ally. This was the first indication to Byrnes that Roosevelt's endorsement was something less than total. Byrnes flatly refused to approach Hillman.

Hannegan called a meeting of the Democratic National Committee for Monday afternoon. He asked Byrnes to meet him at the Blackstone Hotel as soon as the committee meeting was over. When Byrnes arrived, Hannegan informed him that Edward J. Flynn violently opposed him. He said that Flynn was absolutely certain that Roosevelt supported Truman. In addition, Hannegan informed Byrnes that Flynn, Hillman and Phil Murray, the president of the CIO, were coming to Hannegan's suite at the Blackstone for dinner before which they would talk to the president.

Byrnes, who wanted to avoid the others, departed for his own suite at the Stevens. A few hours later, Hannegan asked Leo Crowley, a close friend of Byrnes, to tell him about their conversation with the president. According to Hannegan, Hillman told the president that organized labor would oppose Byrnes because of his hold-the-line order on wages and Flynn told the president that Byrnes would cost the president 200,000 Negro votes in New York. Finally, Hannegan said the president was withdrawing his support of Byrnes and was now in favor of Truman. Crowley promptly informed Byrnes, who was badly shaken by this third-hand message from the president.

At face value, the president's abrupt change of mind amounted to nothing more than a weary man yielding to the importunities of Sidney Hillman and Edward Flynn. There are, however, substantial reasons for believing that FDR, Hannegan and Kelly concocted a carefully staged ploy to eliminate Byrnes from the race. The essence of this ploy was the pretense for a few days that Byrnes was the president's choice. There are three authoritative accounts of Hannegan's and Kelly's meeting with FDR in his private railroad car, which are remarkably consistent on one point: that Byrnes was not the president's choice.

Admiral Leahy's account, which was based on his notes made at the time, reads in part:

> We reached Chicago shortly after noon, July 15, where during a service stop some high political leaders of the Democratic Party boarded the train and conferred with the President. . . . In talking with Roosevelt, I frequently slipped in a strong recommendation for his favorable consideration of Byrnes. On the Presidential car, and in Roosevelt's presence, we talked frequently about our preferences for the second highest post on the Democratic ticket—that is, all of us except the President himself. After we left Chicago, he gave us the surprising information that he had recommended Senator Harry Truman of Missouri, for Vice President.[27]

If Roosevelt had decided on Byrnes at his meeting with Hannegan and Kelly, it is virtually inconceivable that he would not have informed Leahy.

Judge Samuel I. Rosenman had been FDR's principal speech writer since his 1928 campaign for governor. His account reads in part:

When we reached Chicago on Saturday, July 15, the
President's train was shunted into the freight yards before being
switched to the tracks going west. There Hannegan came aboard.
Mrs. Roosevelt and I were finishing lunch with the President in
the dining compartment of his private car. We excused ourselves,
and left Hannegan alone with the President for about an hour.

He had come to the train to give the President a first-hand
report on the convention—particularly to tell him about the
impasse caused by Truman's determination to support Byrnes and
his refusal to become a candidate himself. . . . Hannegan's job was
to get Byrnes out of the contest and Truman in—so that Wallace
could not win.

As Hannegan left the train, he had Roosevelt's encouragement and support . . .[28]

Judge Rosenman clearly states that FDR was alone with Hannegan. If that was
true, it is not inconceivable that Roosevelt first instructed Mayor Kelly to summon
Byrnes to Chicago and then in private told Hannegan that Truman was his real
preference.

In his introduction to Grace Tully's memoir, Justice William O. Douglas wrote,
"Grace Tully knew the man as no one, apart from his family and Marguerite
LeHand, knew him."[29] Her account of Hannegan's meeting with FDR on that rail-
road car remains the strongest evidence of what FDR and Hannegan had agreed on:

The train stood in the Chicago yards during this
conference and none of us showed ourselves outside. Hannegan
had a lengthy palaver with the Boss and when he came out of the
President's sitting room he was carrying in his hand the letter
naming Douglas or Truman as an acceptable running mate. He
came directly to me. 'Grace, the President wants you to retype
this letter and to switch these names so it will read 'Harry
Truman or Bill Douglas.' ' " The reason for the switch was obvious. By naming Truman first it was plainly implied by the letter
that he was the preferred choice of the President. The
convention took it that way and Truman was nominated.[30]

The week before the convention, Wallace had more delegates than any other
candidate. Hannegan and Kelly were desperate to stop him. Their fear was that in a
three-way race with the opposition divided between Truman and Byrnes, Wallace

would emerge the winner. Hannegan and Roosevelt instinctively knew that if they humiliated Byrnes, the proud South Carolinian would bow out. Who persuaded whom to adopt this stratagem will never be known, but it is highly unlikely that Hannegan deceived Byrnes on his own. The fact that he met with Roosevelt on the railroad car indicates that he was not about to make any move without first checking with the "boss."

After an unsatisfactory telephone discussion with FDR, Byrnes ended his quest for the vice presidency with a letter to the chairman of the South Carolina delegation stating that he did not wish his name to be placed in nomination. On Thursday afternoon, a bitter Byrnes, who never knew the full extent of how he had been betrayed, departed Chicago.

On Friday, July 21, after seven hours, a weary convention gave Truman the nomination on the second ballot. It is difficult to discern Roosevelt's feelings about Truman's nomination. According to his son, James, only the day before the president had seemed indifferent about who his running mate would be.

> Before the exercise began, I was alone with father in his private railroad car. We talked of many things—the war, the family, and politics. At that time, the Democratic Convention in Chicago was wrangling over a vice-presidential nominee. I was struck by Father's irritability over what was happening in Chicago and by his apparent indifference as to whom the Convention selected as his fourth-term running mate. He made it clear that he was resigned to the dumping of Vice President Henry A. Wallace; he felt that Wallace had become a political liability. Although Father did not commit himself, I came away with the distinct impression that he really preferred Justice William O. Douglas as the vice presidential nominee. But he professed not to "give a damn" whether the delegates came up with Justice Douglas, Jimmy Byrnes or Senator Harry Truman.[31]

The single most important decision that Roosevelt made in 1944 was his endorsement of a candidate for the vice presidency. His indifference defies understanding. Afterward, Secretary of the Interior Harold Ickes, who could be as candid as he was caustic, wrote Roosevelt's old friend, Bernard M. Baruch.

I don't feel too happy about what has happened here in Chicago. I don't object to Truman, but I react strongly against the method of his nomination and the seemingly dominating position that the corrupt city bosses now have in the Democratic National organization.

I didn't see Jimmy Byrnes while he was here. I put in several calls, one or two of them personally, but I can understand it if Jimmy felt too bruised in spirit not to want to be bothered to talk even with one who sympathized deeply with him and whose only object was to tell him so.[32]

Who were those "corrupt city bosses"? Baruch knew that Ickes was referring to Ed Kelly, the boss of Chicago, Ed Flynn, the boss of the Bronx, and Bob Hannegan, whom the other two had handpicked to head the Democratic National Committee. In 1944, the era of big city bosses was not yet over, but that summer in Chicago their influence was vastly inflated because the leader of the Democratic Party, Franklin Roosevelt, lacked the strength and vitality to dominate the convention.

CHAPTER FOUR

Hopkins and Roosevelt

"The fact of the matter was—and this was later confirmed by Hopkins to Churchill—that a distinct change had come about in the character of his relationship with the President."

ROBERT E. SHERWOOD

author of *Roosevelt and Hopkins, An Intimate History*

Of all those in Franklin Roosevelt's inner circle during the war, Harry Lloyd Hopkins was the most influential and the most interesting. The two men had known each other from the time when Roosevelt, as governor of New York, had appointed Hopkins chairman of the Temporary Emergency Relief Administration. Before the war in Europe convinced him to seek a third term, Roosevelt had encouraged Hopkins to run for president in 1940. In 1937, however, Hopkins' career in government appeared to be over. He was diagnosed with cancer and had a large part of his colon removed. For the rest of his life, Hopkins was unable to absorb fats and proteins properly, which left him chronically undernourished and frail.

Hopkins had inherited his mother's sharp features and penetrating eyes. His slender, almost emaciated body concealed a passionate, caring nature and a razor-sharp mind. With good reason, many considered him abrasive. He liked to confront prominent people whom he had just met with questions that were provocative, if not rude. At his first meeting with Churchill, he wanted to know whether the rumor that Churchill did not like America, Americans or Roosevelt was true. At a time when the Russian people were making great sacrifices in their war with Nazi Germany, Hopkins had angered Charles E. Bohlen by asking him whether he was a member of the anti-Soviet clique in the State Department. Bohlen, who later would accompany Roosevelt to Teheran and Yalta, learned to admire Hopkins, of whom he wrote, "As I got to know Hopkins and saw the depth of his devotion to Roosevelt, how he pulled himself from his sick bed day after day to help the President, I became a staunch admirer of this brilliant, moody man . . ."[1]

Before 1941, Hopkins had been a controversial domestic figure largely unknown outside of America. He had no way of knowing that during the most momentous years of the twentieth century, he would be called on to play a historic role in the foreign relations of the United States.

World War II had commenced on September 1, 1939, with the German invasion of Poland. The Polish armed forces resisted the Nazi blitzkrieg with great courage, but any hope of a prolonged resistance was shattered when Russian forces, in close collaboration with the Germans, invaded eastern Poland. Great Britain and France declared war against Germany on September 3. France immediately mobilized its highly vaunted army of over 4 million.

The BEF (British Expeditionary Force) began to move to France on September 4. Originally consisting of two corps of two divisions each, it was later reinforced with eight more divisions. The BEF was deployed along the France-Belgium border between the French First Army and the French Seventh Army.

On the night of May 10, 1940, Hopkins had dined with Roosevelt at the White House. FDR noticed how miserable Hopkins was feeling and invited him to spend the night. It was the beginning of his three-and-a-half-year residence at the White House as the president's private guest. That night they had much to talk about. Before dawn that day, Germany had launched a massive invasion of Holland, Belgium and Luxembourg. Over the next three weeks, with mounting dismay, the two of them read and listened to the latest reports from the Battle of France. It soon became apparent that the French army was in a state of near collapse. By the last week of May, most of the best divisions in the British Army were trapped in the northwest corner of France near the port of Dunkirk.

On June 4, Churchill spoke to the House of Commons about the evacuation from Dunkirk. He described the "miracle of deliverance" in words that Roosevelt and Hopkins would never forget:

> When a week ago today I asked the House to fix this afternoon as the occasion for a statement, I feared it would be my hard lot to announce the greatest military disaster in our long history.
>
> • • •
>
> A miracle of deliverance, achieved by valor, by perseverance, by perfect discipline, by faultless service, by resource, by skill, by unconquerable fidelity, is manifest to us all.
>
> • • •
>
> The Royal Air Force engaged the main strength of the German Air Force, and inflicted upon them losses of at least four to one; and the Navy, using nearly 1000 ships of all kinds, carried over 335,000 men, French and British, out of the jaws of death and shame, to their native land and to the tasks which lie immediately ahead.

Churchill closed his speech with words that belong to the ages:

> We shall go on to the end, we shall fight in France, we shall fight on the seas and oceans, we shall fight with growing confidence and growing strength in the air, we shall defend our island, whatever the cost may be, we shall fight on the beaches, we shall fight on the landing grounds, we shall fight in the fields and in the streets, we shall fight in the hills; we shall never surrender.[2]

In August, Hopkins was sure that his service to his country was about to end. In a private letter to the president, written in long hand, he revealed himself in a way that he seldom did.

> . . . I have told you little that is in my mind and heart as I leave the government's service . . . I think of the things that have

made my years with you the happiest time of my life. The first
exciting days—the exaltation of being part of government—our
first formal dinner at the White House when I met Cardozo . . .
And one day you went to church with me when the going wasn't
so good—and life seemed ever so dark . . . And there was always
New Year's Eve—and the warm glow of "Auld Lang Syne"—with
champagne. That's about the only time we got champagne
around your house. Or am I wrong? . . . I've always been getting
on and off trains—and I saw America and learned to know its
people. I like them . . . And one day two nice people came to visit
you—he was a king—and I hope will be for a long time and she
was a Scotch girl who got to be a queen. And after dinner that
night you and Missy and I talked it all over till 2 A.M. . . . All
these things I think of—and Mac and Steve and Tommy and Ben
and Rex and Felix and Sam and Missy—I know they are important because I remember them—and they are good.

   This letter is simply to say that I have had an awfully good
time—and to thank you very much. And by the way—my
weather bureau tells me that it will be fair tomorrow.[3]

If Hopkins thought there would be no more challenges in his life, he could not
have been more mistaken. There was some improvement in his health. In late
November 1940, Joseph P. Kennedy resigned as ambassador to the Court of St.
James's, which Roosevelt had done nothing to discourage. Kennedy's departure
would soon create an opportunity for Hopkins in the diplomatic field which he
could never have imagined.

   On December 2, Hopkins joined the president and his immediate staff for a
Caribbean cruise on the U.S.S. *Tuscaloosa*. The White House announced that the
purpose of the cruise was to inspect recently acquired base sites in the Caribbean,
but those familiar with the president's vacation habits thought that "the main business of each day would be fishing, basking in the sun and spoofing with cronies."[4]

   It was not quite the lighthearted cruise that the president had planned. On the
morning of December 9, a Navy seaplane delivered the White House pouch
bulging with documents. Among these was a letter of some 4000 words which historians regard as the single most important communication that Churchill ever
sent Roosevelt. After giving Roosevelt his appreciation of the war situation, includ-

ing the threat posed by the Empire of Japan, the British prime minister explained the British plight:

> The moment approaches when we shall no longer be able to pay cash for shipping and other supplies. While we will do our utmost and shrink from no proper sacrifice to make payments across the exchange, I believe you will agree that it would be wrong in principle and mutually disadvantageous in effect if, at the height of this struggle, Great Britain were to be divested of all salable assets so that after victory was won with our blood, civilization saved and time gained for the United States to be fully armed against all eventualities, we should stand stripped to the bone. Such a course would not be in the moral or economic interests of either of our countries. . . . Moreover I do not believe the Government and people of the United States would find it in accordance with the principles which guide them, to confine the help which they have so generously promised only to such munitions of war and commodities as could be immediately paid for. You may be assured that we shall prove ourselves ready to suffer and sacrifice to the utmost for the Cause, and that we glory in being its champion. The rest we leave with confidence to you and your people, being sure that ways and means will be found which future generations on both sides of the Atlantic will approve and admire.[5]

Churchill's words profoundly affected Roosevelt and Hopkins. Two days later, Lord Lothian, the highly regarded British ambassador to the United States, unexpectedly died in Washington of uremic poisoning. A diplomatic void now existed in both countries. Convinced that Hitlerism was a clear and present danger to the United States, and certain that Britain was defending Western civilization against a deadly evil, Roosevelt conceived of a way to save Britain without a declaration of war. On the evening of December 29, he presented his case to the American people in a fireside chat by a national radio hookup from the diplomatic reception room of the White House. He asked the American people to do what no other president had asked of them before:

> Certain facts are self-evident. In a military sense Great Britain and the British Empire are today the spearhead of resist-

ance to world conquest. And they are putting up a fight which will live forever in the story of human gallantry.

. . .

We are planning our own defense with the utmost urgency and in its vast scale we must integrate the war needs of Britain and the other free nations that are resisting aggression. This is not a matter of sentiment . . . it is a matter of realistic, practical military policy . . .

. . .

We must be the great arsenal of democracy. For us this is an emergency as serious as war itself. We must apply ourselves to our tasks with the same resolution, the same sense of urgency, the same spirit of patriotism and sacrifice as we would show were we at war.

We have furnished the British great material support and we will furnish far more in the future.[6]

Hopkins had contributed the most memorable line of the president's talk. "We must be the great arsenal of democracy." Roosevelt would carry the American people, and ultimately the Congress, with him in his decision to save Britain. The Lend-Lease bill, which the president submitted to Congress in January, would provide Britain with virtually unlimited arms and supplies without requiring cash payments.

Roosevelt was anxious to be in closer personal contact with Churchill. Early in January, he decided to send Hopkins to London. Even though Hopkins had been eager to go, Roosevelt had hesitated with good reason. Hopkins' health was always a concern. He lacked experience in foreign affairs. He had a tendency to be curt and even abrasive. If he were to rile Churchill, Anglo-American relations might suffer.

Ultimately, Roosevelt sent Hopkins to London with his blessings, but without any written instructions. Hopkins' mission was an undoubted triumph. In five weeks, he and Churchill forged a friendship of historic importance. It was a turning point in Hopkins' life. Before this mission to London, he had been a domestic political figure largely unknown outside the United States. Afterward, Hopkins was known all over the world. After the war, Churchill wrote of Hopkins:

He was the most faithful and perfect channel of communication between the president and me. But far more than that, he was for several years the main prop and animation of Roosevelt himself. Together these two men, the one a subordinate without public office, the other commanding the mighty republic, were capable of taking decisions of the highest consequence over the whole area of the English-speaking world.[7]

Throughout the next three years, Hopkins remained Roosevelt's closest confidant and his most important foreign policy advisor. At the Teheran Conference in late 1943, Hopkins perhaps reached the apex of his career. Charles E. Bohlen, a rising star in the State Department, would later write:

After the Russian dinner—as I later heard—Hopkins went to see Churchill at the British Embassy and told him that he was fighting a losing battle in trying to delay the invasion of France. The view of the United States about the importance of an assault across the Channel had been firmly fixed for many months, Hopkins said, and the Soviet view was equally adamant. There was really little Churchill could do, Hopkins emphasized, in advising the prime minister to yield with grace. It is still not clear whether Hopkins acted under Roosevelt's instructions in going to Churchill. I was not privy to Roosevelt's talks with Hopkins or with Harriman. But at that time Roosevelt was relying more and more on Hopkins, virtually to the exclusion of others. At Teheran, Hopkins' influence was paramount.[8]

If 1943 was the apex of Hopkins' influence with the president, 1944 was the nadir. What happened has never been fully explained. Only Franklin Roosevelt knew the complete explanation and he never revealed it. The most dramatic manifestation of Hopkins' fall from grace was the president's decision not to take him to the second Quebec Conference in September 1944. Hopkins had been present at every previous meeting with Churchill. Churchill was sorely disappointed to learn of Hopkins' exclusion and was anxious to know the reasons behind it. Afterward, Churchill wrote of Hopkins' absence:

We landed at Halifax on September 10, and reached Quebec the following morning. The President and Mrs.

Roosevelt, who were our guests, had arrived just before us, and the President waited at the station to greet me.

• • •

The President had with him Leahy, Marshall, King and Arnold. But this time, alas, there was no Harry Hopkins. He had sent me a telegram just before I left England: "Although I am now feeling much better, I still must take things easy, and I therefore feel that I should not run the risk of a setback in health by attempting to fight the Battle of Quebec on the Plains of Abraham, where better men than I have been killed." I was not then aware of the change in the character of his relationship with the president . . .[9]

After the conference ended, Churchill journeyed to Hyde Park with his wife as guests of President and Mrs. Roosevelt. It was there that Hopkins made his initial appearance. Churchill later wrote of Roosevelt's coolness.

I lunched there (Hyde Park) on September 19. Harry Hopkins was present. He was obviously invited to please me. He explained to me his altered position. He had declined in the favor of the president. There was a curious incident at luncheon, when he arrived a few minutes late and the president did not even greet him.[10]

Eleanor Roosevelt and Eugene Bernard Casey are not often identified with those who sought Harry Hopkins' downfall; yet they both are likely candidates for this role. The only biographer of Hopkins who had the opportunity to interview Mrs. Roosevelt did not do so. In his introduction to *Roosevelt and Hopkins,* Robert E. Sherwood explained: "One name that is conspicuously absent from the list of those that I interviewed is that of Eleanor Roosevelt. . . . I simply could not bring myself to put any questions to her, because her memories are her own, and I felt reluctant to intrude upon any part of them."[11] Even if she had advised her husband to distance himself from Hopkins, it is, of course, by no means certain that she would have revealed this to Sherwood.

Eleanor Roosevelt had known Harry Hopkins from the earliest days of the New Deal. She had admired his work as a passionate champion of the poor. She often had invited him to be a guest at Hyde Park and the White House. When Hopkins lost his second wife, Barbara, to cancer, Mrs. Roosevelt had taken charge of their daughter, Diana, who was only five. In July 1942, after Hopkins had been living at the White House for over two years, he married Louise Macy. Mrs. Roosevelt agreed, albeit reluctantly, that they could remain in the guest quarters. By then her relationship with Hopkins was declining. Ironically, Hopkins had been Eleanor's friend first, but over time he had gravitated toward her husband. Ultimately, he dedicated all of his energy, time and talents to the service of the president. Eleanor keenly felt the loss of his attention. Once Hopkins had warned an attractive young woman, who knew both the president and the First Lady, "Mrs. Roosevelt could freeze if she felt you were succumbing to the President's charm and abandoning her." He knew from personal experience.[12]

During the war, Hopkins' precarious state of health was always a concern. On New Year's Day 1944, he was enjoying a group of friends when he suddenly felt ill. His deteriorating condition led to an operation at the Mayo Clinic on March 29, 1944, for the purpose of allowing his small intestine to function better. The surgery was only marginally successful. From then until July, he was in and out of hospitals and almost never at the White House. Eleanor Roosevelt seems to have concluded that Hopkins physically would never again be able to be her husband's indispensable advisor. After Hopkins' death, she asserted in her autobiography that circumstances were the only reasons for the change in his relationship with her husband.

> It was circumstances that separated them. As I have said, Harry was no longer living in the White House, and in addition he was far from well. He could not carry the active burdens he had once carried. Franklin had so much to do that, no matter how deeply he might have felt, he had no time to keep up any personal relationship that did not also fit in with the demands of his work. This is a hard attitude; nevertheless, it meets the necessities of such a situation.[13]

In her book, she also revealed her distaste for the frivolous side of Hopkins, who loved parties and kept late hours. There was, however, a far more compelling reason why she wanted her husband to distance himself from Hopkins.

Mrs. Roosevelt held well-concealed reservations about Churchill. In November 1942, on her first wartime visit to London, one of Mrs. Roosevelt's first conversations with the British leader had turned unpleasant. Over dinner, she had said that more should have been done to help the Loyalists during the Spanish Civil War. Churchill replied that the two of them would have been the first to lose their heads if the Loyalists had won. Mrs. Roosevelt declared that "losing my head was unimportant."[14] Whereupon Churchill observed, "I don't want you to lose your head and neither do I want to lose mine."[15] When Mrs. Churchill tactfully took Mrs. Roosevelt's side, the prime minister growled, "I have held certain beliefs for sixty years and I'm not going to change now."[16] A month after her return from England, she sat next to Vice President and Mrs. Wallace at a White House dinner. Wallace wrote of their conversation in his diary for December 16:

> At the White House . . . I sat next to Mrs. Roosevelt. She mentioned how exceedingly cold it was staying in the Castle with the mother of King George. She has very little use for Churchill and told Mrs. Wallace about a dinner at which she had spoken out quite strongly against Franco, and Churchill had talked on the other side.[17]

Their first disagreement was slightly humorous and had not lasted for long, but in September 1944, when Churchill was a guest at Hyde Park, she debated him in a serious way. The only witnesses to this unlikely encounter were Admiral William D. Leahy and Laura Delano, a cousin of the president.

Leahy's recollection of their argument was based on his contemporaneous notes:

> The next day, September 19, we had a most interesting lunch at Mrs. Roosevelt's farmhouse, which lies a mile or two east of the main Hyde Park residence. Sitting at a table with Miss Delano, a cousin of the president, Mrs. Roosevelt, and Churchill, I listened to an hour of argument by the latter two on their general attitude toward a reorganization of the world. Mrs. Roosevelt argued with conviction that peace could best be maintained by improving the living conditions of the people in all countries. Churchill, on the contrary, said that his only hope for a durable peace was an agreement between Great Britain and the United

States to prevent international war by the use of their combined forces if necessary. He expressed a willingness to take Russia into the agreement if the Russians wished to join. He did not believe China could be anything but a source of trouble if it should be permitted to join. Churchill presented his case with clarity and conviction.[18]

Their debate could only have confirmed Mrs. Roosevelt's opinion that Churchill would try to thwart her husband's plans for the postwar world. She had been aware since their first meeting in January 1941 that Hopkins was probably closer to Churchill than any of her husband's other advisors. This could not have pleased her.

Hopkins had been told that there were those trying to destroy him because of his friendship with Churchill. In a 1944 Christmas letter to Churchill, he reassured the prime minister of the bond between them, writing, "and you will know with what affection Louie and I send you and Clemmie our warmest Christmas greeting . . . there are some of my countrymen who would destroy me by the assertion that I am your good friend. All I can say is that I am ever so proud that it is so."[19] It is unclear whether Hopkins suspected Mrs. Roosevelt.

Of all those who advised Roosevelt to discard Hopkins, Eugene B. Casey has to be one of the more obscure; however, his long tenure at the White House and his friendships with others more powerful than he gave him greater influence than he ordinarily would have had. He was born in 1904 in Washington, D.C. He attended Penn State College and Georgetown University. Afterward, he had become active in the Democratic Party in Columbia, Maryland, which led to his presidency in a Young Men's Democrat organization. By the time he was thirty-six, he had become wealthy. His land holdings included seven dairy and grain farms in Montgomery County, Maryland. He listed his home address as "New Deal Farms," Gaithersburg, Maryland.

In 1940, Casey served as a delegate from Maryland to the Democratic National Convention. Earlier, he had gone to work for the Farm Credit Administration where he had caught the attention of Secretary of Agriculture Henry A. Wallace. At the convention, Casey strongly supported Wallace to become his party's nominee for vice president.

In February 1941, Casey became executive assistant to the president, whom he advised primarily on agricultural matters. Henry Wallace, who had then been vice president for only a month, almost certainly got this job for Casey. Harry Hopkins had been living at the White House since May 10, 1940. Inevitably, they became acquainted. Casey, however, made little, if any, lasting impression on Hopkins. Robert E. Sherwood, who had access to all of Hopkins' correspondence and memoranda, never once refers to Casey in his 934-page work *Roosevelt and Hopkins.*

Eugene Casey never published an account of his experiences in the White House, which lasted almost four years. Without the diaries of Henry Wallace, it is unlikely that his vendetta against Hopkins would have come to light. On December 2, 1942, Casey shared his suspicions about Hopkins with Wallace, who wrote:

> Gene Casey claimed that there was a cabal between Somervell, Forrestall [*sic*] and Eberstadt with Harry Hopkins in the background manipulating it. He said that these men felt that the Democratic Party needed to be given a completely new line. They felt that the Army should be brought into the Democratic Party in a big way and also certain big business interests. I told Casey . . . that I did not think there was anything in the nature of a cabal and that I didn't agree with him that these men believed in a fascist, military dictatorship for the United States.[20]

Casey continued to be an executive assistant to the president for almost two more years. By the beginning of 1944, his suspicions of Hopkins had hardened into an intense, personal dislike, which he was not reluctant to discuss with the vice president. On January 3, 1944, he met privately with Wallace, who wrote:

> . . . Gene began talking about Harry Hopkins. He gave specific details as to how Hopkins had tried to cut my throat at various times. I have no doubt that Gene is absolutely accurate in reporting this. He said that he had told the President that he has got to get rid of Harry Hopkins. Gene says that Democratic National Committeemen, when they meet here January 22, are going to demand that Hopkins be gotten rid of before the national campaign . . . I told Gene that while I know that Hopkins had been wholeheartedly against me, that I felt he also had been wholeheartedly for winning the war, and that he had worked with the President to good advantage to win the war. Gene came back

and said, "You are a Christian and I love you for it. But you are wrong about your attitude toward Harry. He is selfish and a no-good and I am going to get him . . ."[21]

Although Wallace had been Casey's friend and mentor, Casey deserted Wallace at the 1944 Democratic Convention. Reflecting on the events of the convention, Wallace wrote: "Gene Casey was working steadily with Ed Flynn to knife me . . . Flynn, Kelly, Hague, Walker, Casey, Jonathan Daniels, and practically the entire White House-National Committee ménage threw everything they had at me, including such picayunish things as not letting the Iowa boys have tickets on Friday . . ."[22]

Since Casey and Flynn had worked together to knife Wallace, it is plausible that earlier they had worked together to knife Hopkins. Flynn had his own reasons for wanting Hopkins out of the picture. When Flynn was chairman of the Democratic National Committee, Hopkins had been Roosevelt's alter ego at the 1940 Democratic Convention, which also took place in Chicago. Flynn had resented Hopkins' involvement in the political process. He later wrote, "Most people are unable to understand this antipathy of the so-called professional politicians for one like Hopkins, whom they consider an amateur . . . [Hopkins] lacked political background and long experience in dealing with political leaders."[23] In 1944, Flynn wanted FDR's running mate handpicked by a select group of "political leaders," including himself. He was not about to brook any interference from Hopkins.

Casey's intrigues against Hopkins seemingly ended in the autumn of 1944 when he resigned as executive assistant to the president to become an officer in the United States Navy Reserve. Eugene Casey remained an enigmatic figure for the rest of his life. In 1947, he pleaded no contest to evading $70,000 in federal income taxes from 1941 to 1943, and served five months of a six-month sentence. In 1951, he received a pardon from President Truman. When he died in 1986 at the age of eighty-two, his estate was estimated at $210 million. He had made this massive fortune in Maryland real estate.

One of Casey's daughters believes that if her father had any private papers that would shed light on his years at the White House, her stepmother, Betty Brown Casey, now owns them; however, her stepmother, through her attorney, has indicated that "she does not want the privacy of her husband's papers disturbed."[24] This same daughter recalled that her father and Ed Flynn were great pals. If Casey succeeded in turning FDR away from Hopkins, it was most likely with Flynn's help.

In October 1944, Hopkins and Roosevelt were reconciled to the extent that Hopkins was restored as FDR's chief advisor on foreign policy. Robert E. Sherwood attributes Hopkins' surprising comeback to a single incident on October 4. On that day Roosevelt had drafted a brief cable to Churchill regarding the forthcoming Moscow meeting between Churchill and Stalin. In this cable, Roosevelt had merely wished Churchill every success in his meeting with the Russian leader. In light of the Quebec Conference, which Stalin had not attended, Hopkins thought "every success" implied that Churchill had authority to speak for the president. When Hopkins learned that this message was about to go out over the wires of the Map Room, "he thereupon took one of the quick and arbitrary actions, far beyond the scope of his own authority . . . he gave orders to the officers on duty in the Map Room that transmission of the president's message to Stalin was to be stopped."[25] Hopkins immediately went to the president, who was upstairs shaving, and expressed his concerns over the implications of the phrase "every success." Realizing that he had almost made a serious mistake, Roosevelt instructed Hopkins to cancel the cable. When Hopkins told him he had already taken the liberty to do so, the president was relieved.

Of those who have written about Roosevelt's and Hopkins' estrangement, Robert E. Sherwood was closer to the event than almost anyone. He knew both men. He had access to all of Hopkins' private papers. In doing his research for *Roosevelt and Hopkins,* Sherwood had three interviews with Churchill, in whom Hopkins had confided at Hyde Park immediately after the second Quebec Conference. It is surprising that Sherwood never reached any definite conclusion about the cause of this estrangement. He does offer some clues.

In a memorandum sent from Quebec, Roosevelt had informed Cordell Hull, his aging secretary of state, that a temporary joint committee would be set up to consider extending Lend Lease aid to Britain after the defeat of Germany and during the war with Japan. Hopkins' name was conspicuously absent from this committee. Of this slight to Hopkins, Sherwood wrote:

> Unpleasant suggestions had reached the president's ears
> to the effect that Hopkins was too thoroughly under the

domination of the British, or of the Russians or the Chinese, to be a reliable representative of American interests in these important negotiations relative to postwar material and economic aid. Of course, similar dark intimations and even worse ones about Hopkins had been reaching Roosevelt ever since the earliest days of the feud* with Harold Ickes in 1933, and Roosevelt had paid no heed to them; but he paid heed to them now.[26]

Since Hopkins had not been at Quebec, where the initial discussion with the British concerning Stage II Lend Lease had taken place, there was a certain logic to excluding him from the Stage II joint committee. The larger question is why had Roosevelt not invited Hopkins to go with him to the summit meeting with Churchill at Quebec. FDR's failure to invite Hopkins remains puzzling. In 1943, Hopkins had accompanied FDR to five summit conferences with Churchill outside the United States. Cordell Hull had attended none except for the first Quebec Conference in August 1943. In September 1944, Roosevelt again invited Hull to go to Quebec. The president was not personally close to his secretary of state. Dean Acheson, who himself would become secretary of state less than five years after Hull, has well described some of the reasons that kept them apart:

> Suspicious by nature, [Hull] brooded over what he thought were slights and grievances, which more forthright handling might have set straight. His brooding led, in accordance with Tennessee-mountain tradition, to feuds. His hatreds were implacable—not hot hatreds, but long cold ones. In no hurry to "get" his enemy, "get" him he usually did. Mr. Hull's feuds grew out of his relations with President Franklin Roosevelt. The natures of the two men being what they were, their relations were bound to be difficult.[27]

---

* The Ickes-Hopkins feud had originated ten years earlier during the Great Depression. Ickes had resented Hopkins' influence with the president as well as Hopkins' ability to outmaneuver Ickes in gaining money and publicity in their somewhat uncoordinated efforts to help the poor.

At the first Quebec conference, the British had found Hull's presence unhelpful. Sir Alexander Cadogan, the permanent under secretary of the British Foreign Office, kept a secret diary in which he revealed his feelings about Hull. "Friday, 20 August . . . The P.M. went off fishing all today, with the President. Cordell Hull arrived about lunch time, and Anthony and I had a long session with him this afternoon. A dreadful old man—vaguer and wordier than Norman Davis, and rather pig-headed, but quite a nice old thing, I dare say."[28]

Even though Roosevelt repeatedly urged Hull to go to the second Quebec conference, he declined because of exhaustion, which was no doubt real. In view of Hopkins' close relationship with Churchill and Hull's limitations, Hopkins would have been far more acceptable to the British. Roosevelt's decision to distance himself from Harry Hopkins before the second Quebec Conference did not affect Hopkins' loyalty to the president; however, it was perhaps symptomatic of Roosevelt's failing judgment, which would soon harm his relationship with Winston Churchill.

CHAPTER FIVE

Churchill and Roosevelt

"In the last eighteen months of Roosevelt's life, I thought the open heartedness diminished."

JOHN COLVILLE

private secretary to Churchill

W hen the twentieth century ended, countless historians acclaimed Winston Leonard Spencer Churchill and Franklin Delano Roosevelt as its two greatest statesmen. The British prime minister and the American president will always be identified with the Second World War during which they forged an unconquerable alliance. Almost a year before Pearl Harbor, Roosevelt had sent Harry L. Hopkins, his closest confidant, to see Churchill, who would never forget Hopkins' words.

> With gleaming eye and quiet, constrained passion he said: "The President is determined that we shall win the war together. Make no mistake about it. He has sent me here to tell you that at all costs and by all means he will carry you through, no matter what

happens to him – there is nothing he will not do so far as he has
human power."[1]

If the war had not yet been won by 1944, the ultimate outcome was certain
unless the Soviet Union made a separate peace with Nazi Germany. Roosevelt and
Churchill already were beginning to plan the shape of the postwar world. Roosevelt's
thoughts increasingly turned to his plans for the future of the British Empire, which
included the subcontinent of India and most of Africa south of the Sahara Desert.
For years, the president had harbored misgivings about the policies of the European
colonial powers. On at least one occasion, he had suggested to Churchill that Britain
return the Crown Colony of Hong Kong to China. Churchill had not taken kindly
to this. The prime minister passionately believed in the greatness of the British
Empire and its benevolent influence on those undeveloped areas of the globe under
the protection of His Majesty's government.

In late February 1944, an ill president, rejecting the advice of the State
Department, confronted Churchill with a dogmatic denunciation of British imperialism in the form of a memorandum prepared by a former secretary of war from the
Hoover administration, Patrick J. Hurley. Hurley was something of an anomaly.
Although he held the rank of an army major general and had undertaken diplomatic assignments for the president, he was neither a career army officer nor a career
diplomat. The president's heavy reliance on Hurley throughout the war in all prob-
ability was due in part to his success in using Harry Hopkins as his special envoy to
Churchill and Stalin, but it was also due to another less obvious factor. There was
growing tension between the president and the State Department.

The previous December at the second Cairo conference, in a private conversation with his son Elliott, the president had denounced the State Department and at
the same time had extolled the virtues of Pat Hurley. Elliott Roosevelt, who had
been with his father at the Teheran conference, flew into Cairo on Sunday,
December 5, and went directly to the Kirk Villa where his father was staying. Elliott
had been given a minor role in the drafting of a three-power agreement guarantee-
ing the postwar independence of Iran. In the middle of the Teheran conference,
Roosevelt had asked Hurley to draft this agreement with Elliott's help. During their
first conversation at the Kirk Villa, Elliott asked his father whether this agreement
had ever been signed. The following monologue ensued:

Oh yes. Signed, sealed and delivered. And by the way, thanks for what *you* did. That Pat Hurley . . . He did a good job. If anybody can straighten out the mess of internal Chinese policies, he's the man. You know, Elliott, . . . men like Pat Hurley are invaluable. Why? Because they're loyal. I can give him assignments that I'd *never* give a man in the State Department because I can depend on him . . .

You know . . . any number of times the men in the State Department have tried to conceal messages to me, delay them, hold them up somehow, just because some of those career diplomats aren't in accord with what they know I think. They should be working for Winston. As a matter of fact, a lot of the time they *are*. Stop to think of 'em: any number of 'em are convinced that the way for America to conduct its foreign policy is to find out what the British are doing and then copy that . . . I was told six years ago to clean out that State Department. It's like the British Foreign Office. They have a man there, his title is Permanent Under Secretary. He's Permanent Under Secretary if the government is Tory, or if it's Labor, or if it's Liberal. Makes no difference. There he is: Permanent. That's our State Department. So there are men like Pat Hurley, and what they do is twice as valuable. The only thing about Pat is, he has to be told what to do. If he's told, he'll do it. And he'll do it faithfully and well.[2]

When Dean Acheson was an assistant secretary of state, Hurley's memorandum denouncing British imperialism was circulated among senior officials of the State Department including Acheson. Much later, Acheson expressed his views of both Hurley and his memorandum with obvious distaste:

Patrick J. Hurley, the former Oklahoma cowboy who struck it rich . . . was home for consultation. Trouble moved with him like a cloud of flies around a steer. Handsome, vain and reckless, he boasted of lethal speed on the draw in the old days in the West and gave ample evidence of seeking equally simplistic answers to complicated problems in this present mission . . .

I had had my own troubles with Hurley in 1944 when, after being invalided out of active military service, he was attached to the Middle East Supply Center. Then, as this time, he had returned to Washington breathing charges about the misuse of lend-lease goods, chiefly that they were being distributed in Iran by the British. This was correct, since British Forces held

Southern Iran and the exigencies of war prevented the presence of Americans. When that factor was eliminated by victory in North Africa, Americans handled lend-lease to Iran. Another charge deplored Russian and British imperialism and urged that the United States disassociate itself from and supplant this by bringing the message of democracy. Hurley's memorandum was sent to Mr. Hull for comment and by him to various of us for reply. I was, perhaps, too brusque with Hurley's proposal to bring democracy to occupied Iran, describing it in the phrase of one of my assistants as "messianic globaloney" which might await the end of the war against Hitler and Mussolini in which we and our criticized allies were cooperating.[3]

To note that Hurley "deplored . . . British imperialism" was an understatement. Hurley's more vehement statements read:

> The American people, single-mindedly devoted to independence and liberty, are fighting today not to save the imperialisms of other nations . . .

· · ·

> The imperialism of Germany, Japan, Italy, France, Belgium, Portugal and The Netherlands will, we hope, end or be radically revised by this war. British imperialism seems to have acquired a new life. This appearance, however, is illusory. What appears to be a new life of British imperialism is the result of the infusion, into its emaciated form, of the blood of productivity and liberty from a free nation through lend lease. British imperialism is also being defended today by the blood of the soldiers of the most democratic nation on earth. The names of the imperialistic nations are sufficient to indicate that a large part of the world's population is still committed to the principles of imperialism. These names also indicate the opposition that will be encountered by any effort that has for its purpose the establishment of democracy in nations that are now subjected to the rule of imperialistic nations. We are approaching the irrepressible conflict between worldwide imperialism and worldwide democracy.

· · ·

> In the quarter of a century which his intervened [since
> World War I] the processes of both eastern and western imperial-
> ism set the stage for this new world war.[4]

Hurley may have been attempting to impress Roosevelt, whose antipathy to
colonialism was well known, or he may have been simply articulating his own con-
victions. But in any case, his statements were bound to be offensive to Churchill.

To compare British imperialism with German, Japanese and Italian
imperialism was nothing short of outrageous. To predict an irrepressible conflict
between Britain, as the leader of imperialism, and America, as the leader of democracy, was fantastic. To say that eastern and western imperialism set "the stage for this
new world war" blames Britain as much as Nazi Germany and Imperial Japan. The
president should have relegated Hurley's memorandum to some obscure file in the
State Department. Instead he forwarded it to Churchill with a cover letter in which
he did not disassociate himself from the more invidious parts of Hurley's dicta.
Indeed, Roosevelt suggested his approval of what Hurley had written: "I rather like
his general approach to the care and education of what used to be called 'backward
countries.'"[5] Sending it to Churchill represents, at the least, an inexplicable lapse of
judgment.

Apparently there is no record of Churchill's initial reaction. In any event, he
refrained from an immediate response. When he finally referred to it in May, the
British leader was preoccupied with the preparations for the invasion of France.
Nevertheless, his letter to Roosevelt of May 21 revealed his disdain.

> The General seems to have some ideas about British imperi-
> alism which I confess make me rub my eyes. He makes out, for
> example, that there is an irrepressible conflict between imperial-
> ism and democracy. I make bold, however, to suggest that British
> imperialism has spread and is spreading democracy more widely
> then any other system of government since the beginning of
> time.[6]

If for no other reason, Iran was important to Britain and the United States
because of oil. Indeed, oil had already become a matter of contention between
Churchill and Roosevelt. In a cable to Roosevelt on February 20, Churchill object-

ed to an imminent international oil conference in Washington on postwar oil policy. The prime minister did not mince his words:

> There is apprehension in some quarters here that the United
> States has a desire to deprive us of our oil assets in the Middle
> East on which, among other things, the whole supply of our navy
> depends . . . I am sure these suspicions are entirely unfounded as
> far as the Government of the United States is concerned . . . when
> however it is announced that you are to open a conference upon
> oil in Persia and the Middle East and that the Secretary of State
> is to be the leader of the American Delegation the whole question
> will become one of first magnitude in Parliament . . . interna-
> tional Conferences at the highest level should surely be carefully
> prepared beforehand and I would beg you to consider whether it
> would not be more advisable to proceed as a first step for official
> and technical talks on the lines which had, I understand, already
> been agreed between the State Department and ourselves.[7]

Two days later Roosevelt cabled a harsh response.

> You point to the apprehension on your side that the United
> States desires to deprive you of oil assets in the Middle East. On
> the other hand, I am disturbed about the rumor that the British
> wish to horn in on Saudi Arabian oil reserves.

• • •

> However, in view of the great long range importance of oil
> to the post-war international security and economic arrange-
> ments, it is my firm conviction that these technical discussions
> should take place under the guidance of a group at Cabinet level
> and I cannot, therefore, change my position in this regard . . . It
> is my view that all of the discussions should take place in
> Washington and that, in order that the broadest possible under-
> standings may be reached, there should be no limitations on the
> petroleum problems to be discussed.[8]

Although Churchill drafted his own cables, Roosevelt usually relied on the State Department or his staff to draft his cables. The wording of this cable was strictly Roosevelt's.

The single most difficult issue of the entire war between the Western democracies and the Soviet Union had already impinged on the Churchill-Roosevelt relationship. This issue was whether Poland would be an independent state free of Soviet control.

Charles B. Bohlen had been a member of the American delegation at the Teheran conference. "Chip" Bohlen, then thirty-nine, was a seasoned foreign service officer with a fluency in the Russian language and with an exceptional understanding of Soviet policy. At Teheran, he was Roosevelt's interpreter at all meetings with Stalin, which included their private discussions. One of their off-the-record conversations concerned the future boundary between Poland and Russia. Stalin was determined that the "Curzon Line" would be the boundary. This line had been casually created by British Prime Minister Lloyd George and formally made part of a note on July 11, 1920, from the British secretary of state for foreign affairs, Lord Curzon (George Nathaniel Curzon), to the Russian government. The Curzon Line, however, had never been recognized by either the Polish or the Russian governments. The 1920 war between Poland and Bolshevik Russia ended with a decisive Polish victory on the Vistula River. Subsequently on March 18, 1921, the Soviet governments of Russia, the Ukraine and Byelorussia signed the Treaty of Riga and unconditionally recognized a permanent boundary between Poland and Russia. It was situated almost one hundred miles east of the Curzon Line.

During this off-the-record conversation, Bohlen and Averell Harriman were the only other Americans in the room with Stalin and Roosevelt. According to Bohlen,

> Roosevelt noted that a presidential election was coming up in 1944, and while he personally did not wish to run again, he might have to if the war was still in progress. He went on to say that there were some six or seven million Americans of Polish extraction, and he did not wish to lose their votes. Therefore, while he personally agreed with Stalin's general view that Poland's frontiers should be moved to the west, he hoped that Stalin would understand why the President could not take part . . . in any such arrangements.[9]

This private dialogue between Roosevelt and Stalin dismayed both Bohlen and Harriman. Harriman "felt the crucial flaw in Roosevelt's approach . . . was that once the Red Army had taken physical possession of Poland and other neighboring countries it might well be too late for a negotiated settlement."[10]

For the eleven months before the presidential election, Roosevelt studiously avoided any public statements that might antagonize Polish American voters. While Poland's boundary with Russia was a serious concern to both countries, the vital issue was whether the people of Poland would be allowed the freedom to choose their own form of government. On all aspects of Polish-Soviet disputes, Roosevelt's inclination was to avoid any confrontation with Stalin. Churchill was prepared to argue with force and passion that it was in Poland's long-range best interest to cede that part of Poland east of the Curzon Line in exchange for new territories in East Prussia and in Germany itself. He was not prepared, however, to acquiesce in Russia's unilateral annexation of eastern Poland. On March 21, Churchill sent Roosevelt the text of his telegram to Stalin, which made this position clear.

> I shall have very soon to make a statement to the House of Commons about the Polish position. This will involve my saying that the attempts to make an arrangement between the Soviet and Polish Governments have broken down; that we continue to recognize the Polish Government, with whom we have been in continuous relations since the invasion of Poland in 1939; that we now consider all questions of territorial change must await the armistice or peace conference of the victorious powers; that in the meantime we can recognize no forcible transferences of territory.[11]

Churchill and Roosevelt's first conference in August 1941, had produced the Atlantic Charter, which stated the basic policies of Great Britain and the United States. It contained eight declarations, the second of which assured the world that the two nations "desire to see no territorial changes that do not accord with the freely expressed wishes of the peoples concerned."[12] Since Roosevelt was publicly committed to the basic principles of the Atlantic Charter, Stalin might well have expected him to send a private message strongly supporting the British position.

When he failed to do so, Stalin, perhaps, sensed Roosevelt's reluctance to confront him. On March 23 the Russian dictator sent Churchill a scornful reply.

> In your message of the 21st March you state that you intend to make a statement in the House of Commons to the effect that all questions of territorial changes must be deferred until the armistice or the peace conference of the victorious powers, and that until then, you cannot recognize any transferences of territories *carried out by force.* I understand this to mean that you represent the Soviet Union as a power hostile to Poland . . . I have no doubt that such a statement of yours will be taken by the peoples of the Soviet Union and world public opinion as an undeserved insult directed at the Soviet Union.
>
> Of course, you are free to make whatever statement you please in the House of Commons—that is your affair. But if you do make such a statement, I shall consider that you have committed an unjust and unfriendly act towards the Soviet Union.[13]

Despite their divergence on vital issues, Churchill and Roosevelt still maintained a reservoir of good will and affection for one another. In April, Churchill was surprised and delighted to receive an unusual gift from Roosevelt. It was a portrait of the president, which prompted Churchill to write, "My dear Franklin, you kindly sent me a portrait of yourself which I like very much and have hung in my bedroom. Here is a tit for your tat. I hope you will accept it, flattering though it be to me, and like it as much as I do yours."[14] Roosevelt warmly replied, "That picture of you I particularly like. So much so that it too becomes an inhabitant of my bedroom wall. I am awfully glad to have it."[15]

On June 5, Allied forces captured Rome, the first Axis capital to fall. Before dawn on June 6, the Allies launched Operation Overlord the long-awaited invasion of France under the supreme command of General Dwight D. Eisenhower. By late June, the Anglo-American armies were no longer in any danger of being driven into the sea. The Allied successes in Italy and France, however, had masked a serious dispute between the British and American chiefs of staff which could only be resolved by Churchill and Roosevelt. On June 28, Churchill sent Roosevelt two cables, the first of which confirmed the existence of a deadlock over the issue of removing substantial forces from northern Italy for the proposed invasion of southern France, which had been given the code name Anvil. The first cable:

> The deadlock between our Chiefs of Staff raises most serious issues. Our first wish is to help General Eisenhower in the most speedy and effective manner. But, we do not think this necessarily involves the complete ruin of all our great affairs in the Mediterranean, and we take it hard that this should be demanded of us.
>
> I am sending you, in a few hours, a very full argument on the whole matter which I have prepared with my own hands, and which is endorsed by the Chiefs of Staff.[16]

In the second cable, the prime minister urged the abandonment of Anvil in twenty-one paragraphs of vintage Churchillian prose. In his concluding paragraphs, he summarized his most powerful arguments:

> Whether we should ruin all hopes of a major victory in Italy and all its fronts and condemn ourselves to a passive role in that theatre, after having broken up the fine Allied army which is advancing so rapidly through that peninsula, for the sake of ANVIL with all its limitations, is indeed a grave question for His Majesty's Government and the President, with the Combined Chiefs of Staff, to decide. For my own part, while eager to do everything in human power which will give effective and timely help to OVERLORD, I should greatly regret to see General Alexander's army deprived of much of its offensive power in northern Italy for the sake of a march up the Rhone Valley, which the Combined Chiefs of Staff have themselves described as unprofitable, in addition to our prime operation of OVERLORD . . . Let us resolve not to wreck one great campaign for the sake of winning the other. Both can be won.[17]

Some have claimed that Churchill tried to impose strategic military decisions on Roosevelt without the benefit of professional military advice. This was hardly true in the case of Anvil. General Sir Harold Alexander, who commanded the Army Group in Italy on June 19, had sent Churchill the following memorandum:

> As I see it, we are on the march to a great victory which has unlimited possibilities. Kesselring's Tenth and Fourteenth Armies are a beaten force but not yet eliminated from the field. . . .

If I can bring them to battle once more, provided that my armies are left intact, I can mass such a powerful force of fresh troops, guns, tanks and air against them that a great break-through into the Po Valley should not only split them in half but finally eliminate Kesselring's two armies. There will then be nothing to stop us marching straight to Vienna, unless of course the Germans send at least ten or more fresh divisions from elsewhere to try to stop us, and I understand that such an enemy course of action is just what is most required to assist our other operations. I believe we have here now the opportunity of inflicting on the German army such a defeat that its repercussions will be unpredictable.[18]

The chief of the Imperial General Staff, General Sir Alan Brooke, was certain that a renewed offensive in Italy would hasten the ultimate Allied victory. His diary for June 28 reads:

And now we have the most marvelous intelligence indicating clearly the importance that Hitler attaches to Northern Italy, his determination to fight for it and his orders to hold a line south of the Pisa-Rimini line whilst this line is being developed. Kesselring's Army is now a hostage to political interference with military direction of operations. It would be madness to fail to take advantage of it and would delay the conclusion of the war.

We spent most of the day drafting a reply, refusing to withdraw forces for a landing in Southern France with the opportunities that lie in front of us. Winston is also sending a wire to the President backing up our message.[19]

All of Churchill's efforts were in vain. Roosevelt had made up his mind before Churchill's second cable of June 28 reached him. The invasion of southern France would proceed as desired by the U.S. chiefs of staff, who were anxious to obtain the port of Marseilles. Churchill made no effort to hide his distress from the president. On July 1 he cabled Roosevelt:

We are deeply grieved by your telegram. There are no differences whatever between my War Cabinet colleagues and the British Chiefs of Staff. The splitting up of the campaign in the

Mediterranean into two operations neither of which can do anything decisive, is, in my humble and respectful opinion, the first
major strategic and political error for which we two have to be
responsible. At Teheran you emphasized to me the
possibilities of a move eastward when Italy was conquered and
mentioned particularly Istria [peninsula of NW Yugoslavia].[20]

Whether Anvil should have been canceled in favor of a major offensive in
northern Italy remains a controversy. After the Allies landed in southern France on
August 15, the German Nineteenth Army of Army Group G conducted a skillful
withdrawal up the valley of the Rhone and by September 14 had found temporary
safety in southern Alsace. It was a relatively easy victory for the Allies, but its strategic importance was limited. The noted British military historian, John Keegan, has
written, ". . . ANVIL had actually diverted the Allies' amphibious fleet and the bulk
of their disposable reserve into an operationally vacant zone and away from the
Balkans, which still bulked so large in importance for (Hitler's) conduct of the war."[21]

If General Alexander's Fifth and Eighth Armies had been able to destroy Field
Marshal Kesselring's armies in the field and then seize the Ljubljana Gap, they might
well have trapped twenty or thirty German divisions in the Balkans. It was also conceivable that General Alexander's two armies could have occupied Austria before the
arrival of the Russians. What is more certain is that any desperate bid to hold northern Italy could only have been achieved at the expense of Hitler's other two fronts.
Anvil did not divert German forces from either northern France or the eastern front.

The people of Poland might well ask whether Churchill's strategy would have
kept the Germans in early August from rushing reinforcements from Italy to
Warsaw, where the Poles would ultimately face annihilation in what came to be
called "the Warsaw Uprising." These reinforcements included the crack Hermann
Goering Panzer Division. If the Polish Underground Army had even been able to
fight the Germans to a stalemate, the Polish government in exile, which was recognized by the British and the Americans, but not by the Russians, could have been
flown into Warsaw. It was not to be.

Both Churchill and Roosevelt were horrified by the huge casualties among
men, women and children as the fighting in Warsaw intensified. Stalin soon revealed
a far different attitude. On August 16, Brooke noted in his diary, "Most of the
C.O.S. [Chiefs of Staff] meeting was taken up with problems as to how to support

the Polish underground rising in Warsaw. The Russians seem to be purposely giving no assistance and the Poles here are naturally frantic."[22] Eight days later, Jock Colville, the youngest of Churchill's private secretaries, wrote,

> The Polish rising in Warsaw is a grim problem. They are fighting desperately against fearful odds. We and the Americans want to help in every way possible; in sending supplies we have been losing up to 30 percent of our aircraft. The Russians are deaf to all pleas and determined to wash their hands of it all. They have even refused to let American bombers land and refuel on Russian airfields if their purpose is to help Warsaw.[23]

Churchill had departed England on August 10 to visit the Italian front and did not return home until August 29. During this time he closely followed events in Warsaw. When the Russians refused to allow American bombers to refuel on Russian airfields, Churchill was livid.

From Siena he sent Roosevelt the draft of a proposed joint cable to Stalin. It read:

> We are most anxious to send American planes from England. Why should they not land on the refueling ground which has been assigned to us behind the Russian lines without inquiry as to what they have done on the way . . . ? We do not try to form an opinion about the persons who instigated this rising which was certainly called for repeatedly by radio Moscow. Our sympathies are, however, for the "almost unarmed people" whose special faith has led them to attack German guns, tanks and aircraft . . . Unless you directly forbid it, therefore, we propose to send the planes.[24]

The following day, in a brief cable, the president dashed Churchill's hope of American support. Roosevelt concluded, "I do not consider it advantageous to the long-range general war prospect for me to join with you in the proposed message to U.J. [Uncle Joe] I have no objection to your sending such a message if you consider it advisable to do so."[25]

Since only the U.S. Eighth Air Force in England had the capacity to supply the Poles on a massive scale, it was pointless for Churchill to act alone. In the last volume of his history of the Second World War, Churchill gave his final judgment on Stalin's indifference to the Polish slaughter:

> I had hoped that the Americans would support us in drastic action . . . I do not remember any occasion when such deep anger was shown by all our members, Tory, Labour, Liberal, alike. I should have liked to say, "We are sending our airplanes to land in your territory, after delivering supplies to Warsaw. If you do not treat them properly all convoys will be stopped from this moment by us." But the readers of these pages in after-years must realize that everyone always has to keep in mind the fortunes of millions of men fighting in a worldwide struggle, and that terrible and even humbling submissions must at times be made to the general aim. I did not therefore propose this drastic step.[26]

Even as the Battle for Warsaw raged, Churchill and Roosevelt journeyed to Quebec for their only conference of 1944. In the previous year, they had met at Casablanca, Washington, Quebec, Cairo, Teheran and again at Cairo. Despite the unexplained absence of Harry Hopkins, the disagreement over Anvil and Roosevelt's failure to back Churchill over Poland, their meeting at Quebec got off to a good start and never became acrimonious.

On September 13, Churchill cabled the deputy prime minister and the War Cabinet, "The Conference has opened in a blaze of friendship. The Staffs are in almost complete agreement already."[27]

Churchill's highest priority at Quebec was to ensure the continuation of Lend Lease to Britain after the German surrender, which many then believed would be before the end of the year. This all-important matter to the British was known as "Stage II." The day after his arrival, Churchill had a letter hand-delivered to Roosevelt:

> One of the most important things I have to discuss with you is Stage II. Would Thursday, 14th, do for that? In which case I hope you could have Henry Morgenthau present. This matter is considered of extreme and vital importance by the British Government, for reasons which are only too painfully apparent.[28]

Their discussions on Thursday concerning Stage II went so well that Churchill was almost euphoric. That night Jock Colville wrote in his diary, "While going to bed the P.M. told me some of the financial advantages the Americans had promised us. 'Beyond the dreams of avarice,' I said. 'Beyond the dreams of justice,' he replied."[29] The prime minister failed to mention that he had not gotten anything in writing.

Churchill and Roosevelt did produce a highly significant aide-mémoir at Hyde Park a few days after leaving Quebec. This document "committed the United States and Great Britain to full collaboration . . . in developing TUBE ALLOYS for military and commercial purposes."[30] TUBE ALLOYS were the British code words for all aspects of atomic energy, including the yet untested atomic bomb. Whatever Roosevelt's motive may have been, it could only strengthen post-war Anglo-American relations.

When Roosevelt was reelected on November 7, no one was more pleased than Churchill. He promptly dispatched a cable to the president telling him, "I always said that a great people could be trusted to stand by the pilot who weathered the storm. It is indescribable relief to me that our comradeship will continue and will help bring the world out of misery."[31] Churchill's undoubted affection for Roosevelt would soon be put to the test.

At Quebec, Churchill had informed Roosevelt and Morgenthau that the British Government considered Stage II a matter of "extreme and vital importance." He was sure that he had won their support. Two months later, Roosevelt reversed himself. The president had not foreseen the precarious post-war condition of the British economy. By the end of the war, Britain "had lost a quarter of her national wealth."[32] In contrast, America's wartime boom created an economic expansion that would last for a quarter of a century. Roosevelt was apparently swayed by domestic political considerations.

On November 21, Under secretary of State Edward R. Stettinius Jr., who would soon replace Cordell Hull as secretary of state, learned first hand of the president's decision to renege on Stage II. In his calendar notes of that date, Stettinius described the president's thinking as follows:

> Mr. Morgenthau presented to the president the results of the discussions with the British on Stage II of British Lend-Lease.

The President could not understand why it was necessary to make any commitment.

He thought the procedure followed in the past on Lend-Lease requisitions and appropriations was proper. Mr. Morgenthau pointed out that this would not be following through on the commitment made to the prime minister at Quebec . . . He also indicated it was not his desire to have anything made public or any record made that the British would not get help in the future as they had in the past. They must rely on our good will. If the British were promised they could get $6 billion of Lend-Lease next year it would present a very serious political problem . . . I talked to Acheson when I returned to the office. He was disturbed about not giving the British a firm commitment.[33]

The president's failure to carry out his commitment to Churchill clouded Anglo-American relations for the better part of a year. When FDR died suddenly on April 12, 1945, his commitment to Churchill became worthless. On V-J day, August 15, President Truman abruptly terminated the Lend-Lease program. A few weeks afterward, Edward R. Stettinius Jr., the U.S. representative on the Executive Committee of the United Nations Preparatory Commission then meeting in London, lunched with Clement Attlee, the new prime minister, at 10 Downing Street. Attlee told Stettinius that while he recognized that Lend-Lease had to come to an end, it was a tragedy that he and the president had not been able to make a joint announcement.

Furthermore, Roosevelt had used the threat of curtailing Lend-Lease in order to pressure Churchill in a dispute with the British over post-war international air routes. Through their colonies, the British controlled airfields all over the world. It was clear that in the post-war era, American airlines would dominate the skies. In the fall of 1944, an international conference in Chicago tried in vain to reach a mutually satisfactory agreement. One of the most difficult issues involved landing rights on British airfields.

Roosevelt instructed Ambassador John Winant, "Please take the following message personally to Winston and convince him that he has got to come through."[34]

If the conference should end either in no agreement or in an agreement which the American people would regard as preventing the development and use of the great air routes the repercussions would seriously affect many other things. We are doing our best to meet your lend-lease needs. We will face Congress on that subject in a few weeks and it will not be in a generous mood if it and the people feel that the United Kingdom has not agreed to a generally beneficial air agreement. They will wonder about the chances of our two countries . . . working together to keep the peace if we cannot even get together on an aviation agreement.[35]

The British could ill afford to vent their anger publicly, but in private they considered Roosevelt's communication nothing less than blackmail. Ambassador Winant had the hapless task of delivering Roosevelt's ultimatum. Colville's diary describes Winant's distress.

Winant came with a letter containing a telegram from the President about civil aviation. It was pure blackmail, threatening that if we did not give way to certain unreasonable American demands, their attitude about Lease-Lend Supplies would change. Winant was shamefaced about presenting it and didn't want to stay for lunch, but the P.M. said that even a declaration of war should not prevent them having a good lunch.[36]

Colville was well aware of Churchill's concerns over the increasing strain on Anglo-American relations. His diary for November 25 continues, "The Americans are also being tough and even threatening about a number of other things and the P.M. is disturbed at having to oppose them over so many issues."[37] The worst was yet to come.

In December, an open breach between the United States and Great Britain was averted only by the good sense of Hopkins and Churchill. This controversy has largely escaped public notice because none of the participants mentioned it in their memoirs. Ostensibly, this crisis was created by Admiral Ernest J. King, who has been called "the most powerful Naval officer in the history of the United States."[38] For most of the war, he occupied the two most powerful positions in the Navy, Commander in Chief of the United States Fleet (COMINCH) and Chief of Naval Operations (CNO). In the former position, "King was directly responsible to the President and was the principal Naval advisor to the President on the conduct of the war."[39] King was an Anglophobe, which hardly endeared him to the British.

Andrew Browne Cunningham was the most highly decorated admiral in the Royal Navy. In May 1939, he had been appointed Command-in-Chief Mediterranean, a position that he held for the first two and a half years of the war. During his command, the Royal Navy never lost a major battle to the Italian Navy. In March 1942, Churchill decided to send him to Washington to be the representative of the First Sea Lord on the Combined Chiefs of Staff Committee. Cunningham's assessment of Admiral King was based on personal contact during one of the more difficult periods of the war.

> I saw a good deal of Admiral Ernest King, my American opposite number. A man of immense capacity and ability, quite ruthless in his methods, he was not an easy fellow to get on with. . . . On the whole I think Ernest King was the right man in the right place, though one can hardly call him a good cooperator. Not content with fighting the enemy, he was usually fighting someone on his own side as well.[40]

General George C. Marshall, the Army's chief of staff, held a similar opinion of King. Marshall had been selected by President Roosevelt to be chief of staff on September 1, 1939, more than two years before King was named to the top job in the Navy. Early in 1942, the two men recognized that they would have to work in harmony; otherwise one of them would have to go. They were able to form a working relationship, but it was never cordial. Toward the end of his life, Marshall told Forrest C. Pogue, who was working on his biography, "I had trouble with King because he was always sore at everybody. He was perpetually mean."[41]

Although Admiral King was undoubtedly tough and possessed a mean streak, neither Marshall nor anyone else considered him a fool. It is hardly conceivable that the admiral would have overtly infringed on the president's constitutional authority to conduct the foreign affairs of the United States. Yet, on December 8, 1944, it appeared to some that he had done just that.

On December 8, Admiral King had issued a brief, but incisive order to the senior United States Naval commander in the Mediterranean, Vice Admiral H. Kent Hewitt, prohibiting American LSTs from furnishing supplies to British troops in Greece, who were then engaged in desperate fighting with irregular forces known as E.L.A.S., the "Peoples National Army of Liberation," clearly under communist control. Churchill had ordered British intervention because he was determined to prevent E.L.A.S. from seizing power before the Greek people could choose their future government through free and fair elections. King's order threatened to disrupt the British supply lines. Churchill's reaction was prompt and predictable. He was outraged by King's order, which he felt unilaterally abrogated a firm commitment by the president. On August 26, Roosevelt had sent Churchill a cable assuring him that he had no objection to British forces preserving order in Greece after the withdrawal of the German Army, and that American planes would be available to transport British paratroops.

Harry L. Hopkins, who did not live long enough to write his memoirs, wrote a contemporaneous memorandum about his role in getting King's order withdrawn. Hopkins' account, after more than fifty years, remains the only primary source of information about this affair. It reads in part:

> On Saturday Night, December 9, 1944, at about 7 P.M. the White House operator told me that "John Martin" was calling me on the overseas phone. This is the name the Prime Minister uses in his telephone calls.
>
> The connection was very bad and I could not, therefore, know what the Prime Minister was talking about. He sounded as tho he was very angry and stirred up about something and wanted me to do something about it. I got the words "Greece" and "Halifax." Inasmuch as it was impossible to make him understand what I was saying, I told him I would find out about it in the morning.
>
> I then tried to get Halifax on the phone to see if he knew what it was all about but could not reach him.
>
> On Sunday morning I went to the Map Room and saw in the morning news summary a sentence that Admiral King had ordered Admiral Hewitt, our American Commander of the Mediterranean Fleet, not to permit any American LSTs to be used to transfer supplies to Greece. King's actual cable was not available.
>
> I went to see Admiral Leahy about this and told him that I thought Admiral Hewitt was under the command of General Wilson and that it seemed funny to me that Admiral King would issue an order directly to Hewitt without consultation with the Joint Chiefs of Staff or the Combined Chiefs of Staff. I told Leahy that I thought King was getting into the political arena and

that we would undoubtedly hear from the British about it. I told
him, furthermore, that I felt that while we should keep our troops
out of Greece, and let the British do the policing, withdrawing
the LSTs was like walking out on a member of your family who
is in trouble. Under any circumstances, we had told the British
that they could use our airplanes to send their paratroopers into
Greece and the action of Admiral King did not jibe with that. I
told him I thought Admiral King should withdraw his order and
if Admiral King or the Joint Chiefs of Staff thought that such an
order should be issued, the recommendation should be made to
the President and that he should make the decision because it was
in the political sphere. I told Admiral Leahy that irrespective of
the merits of Admiral King's actions, I thought he had gotten off
base from an organization point of view. Leahy agreed with this
and told me that when he saw the message he called King and
told him he thought King had made a mistake, but he did not tell
King to countermand the order.

  While I was with Leahy he called Admiral King up and told
King he was talking to me and we both felt it was a mistake and
Leahy suggested to King that he withdraw the order. King readi-
ly agreed and did so.[42]

Later in the morning, Hopkins received an urgent request to meet Halifax, who
was the British Ambassador. They met at Hopkins' house at 12:30 P.M. His memorandum continues:

  Halifax said he was sure Churchill was planning to send a
very strong protest to the President . . . I told Halifax I hoped
Churchill would not send the message; that I was sure the
President knew nothing about it; that the matter was all cleared
up anyway and that I knew instructions had gone to Admiral
Hewitt countermanding the previous order and I thought it
would just make trouble if Churchill submitted a protest.[43]

That same afternoon, Halifax drafted a personal and secret cable for the immediate attention of the prime minister. It was dispatched at 2:44 P.M. Washington
time. The cable read in part, "Harry has just told me that King had agreed to
cancel his order to Hewitt about LSTs for Greece, and asked me to let you know.

King had apparently issued the order on his own. Harry hopes that if this matter is now satisfactorily settled it may be possible to leave well enough alone."[44]

The next day, Churchill sent Hopkins a response which showed how highly he regarded the latter's judgment. Churchill cabled, "I naturally accept your advice for which I asked and have canceled the telegram I had prepared for the president."[45] Churchill distributed copies of the cable to Hopkins, to His Majesty the King, to the foreign secretary, to Sir E. Bridges, and to General Ismay (Hastings Lionel Ismay). Sir Edward Bridges was secretary of the Cabinet. Ismay was chief of staff to Churchill and the main channel of communication between Churchill and the chiefs of staff. Churchill had not treated King's order as some trivial misunderstanding.

The president was in Warm Springs, Georgia, on the date that Admiral King issued his order that partially cut the British supply line to Greece. There is no evidence that King sought or received the president's approval of this specific order; however, Hopkins was absolutely right that this order involved a political decision that could only be made at the highest level of government. King surely understood this and it is safe to assume that he would not have issued this order without having received some prior authorization from his commander-in-chief.

Churchill seems not to have suspected Roosevelt's involvement. On the same day that he dispatched his personal cable to Hopkins, he sent him a copy of the cable originally intended for the president.

> We have been attacked by forces far stronger than were anticipated, but we have not diverged in the slightest degree from the policy towards Greece agreed upon by you and me.
>
> If, now that we are heavily engaged, orders are given by the United States which have the effect of partially cutting our lines of communications and impeding reinforcement and maintenance of our troops, this might produce a disaster of the first magnitude.
>
> I cannot believe that you have seen these orders. If such were your intentions, I am sure you would have let me know in good time in what way I had diverged from our agreement.[46]

Elliott Roosevelt, the president's second son, knew more than Churchill. In November, Elliott, a colonel in the Army Air Force, had flown to Washington from

England. The White House usher's diary for Wednesday, November 15, shows that Colonel Roosevelt arrived at 4:20 P.M. on that date as one of two house guests. The next reference to him in the diary shows that he departed the White House at 2:25 P.M. on Friday, November 17. Elliott later described a conversation with his father on the morning of his departure.

> He waved me to a chair; he was scowling over some official dispatches; the morning newspapers had been irritably crumpled on the floor. For some minutes he read, exclaiming every now and then, muttering his dissatisfaction. When he looked up, my eyebrows were raised in curiosity.
> "Greece" he said, "British troops. Fighting against the guerrillas who fought the Nazis for the last four years." He made no attempt to conceal his anger . . . . "How the British can dare such a thing!" Father cried. "The lengths to which they will go to hang on to the past!" . . . "I wouldn't be surprised," he went on, "if Winston had simply made it clear he was backing the Greek Royalists. That would be only in character. But killing Greek guerrillas! Using British soldiers for such a job!"
> "Probably using American Lend-Lease equipment to do it, too." I reminded him.
> "I'll find out about *that*," Father said. And then, "though I don't suppose there's too much I can do about it."
> "A public statement?" "Condemning the British." He shook his head, "Not now. Time enough to raise it when I see Winston in February. And anyway . . ." and his scowl disappeared.
> "Anyway what?" He changed the subject abruptly.[47]

In actuality, the British had not yet engaged the communist guerrilla forces; however, earlier that morning the State Department had apprised the president of secret British contingency plans. The dispatch which had incited Roosevelt's wrath was a combined summary dated November 17, 1944, of recent telegrams to the secretary of state.

It read in part:

Greece   7 A.M.

> British report a plot or a coup d'etat was discovered and the situation in Greece is most critical. SAC has ordered all British

troops there to remain and use force required to crush ELAS troops. (Caserta 1336)

MacVeagh reports that the Embassy lacks information that direct action against the British-supported Government in Greece is contemplated at this time.[48]

SAC was Supreme Allied Commander Mediterranean, General Sir H. Maitland Wilson. Caserta was a town northeast of Naples where Wilson had his headquarters. MacVeagh was Lincoln MacVeagh, the American ambassador to Greece, who was well known to Roosevelt.

That same morning, the president had an 11:45 A.M. appointment with Secretary of the Navy James Forrestal and Admiral Ernest J. King. As a policy Roosevelt never allowed minutes to be kept of his private meetings with Admiral King or General Marshall and there is no reason to think that he deviated from that policy on this occasion. King never kept a diary, but Forrestal did. That Friday, Forrestal saw the president twice, once in the morning with Admiral King and once in the afternoon with the Cabinet. Although his diary makes no reference to the morning meeting, it does refer to a specific directive that Roosevelt gave to his entire Cabinet. Forrestal wrote, "General Policies as regards the rest of Europe. (a) Avoid use of our troops for intra country disturbances."[49] Clearly, Roosevelt was preoccupied with events in Greece, the only recently liberated country having serious intra-country disturbances. If he was adamantly opposed to the use of U.S. troops, he would also have been opposed to the use of the U.S. Navy. Based on all the circumstances, it is highly probable that on Friday, November 17, the president of the United States gave Admiral King and Secretary of the Navy Forrestal secret instructions which culminated in King's order of December 8 to cut off supplies to British forces in Greece.

The finest hour in the Churchill-Roosevelt relationship had been in January, 1941, when Roosevelt had sent Hopkins to London to assure Churchill that the president would do anything within his power to save Britain. The darkest hour in their relationship had been in November 1944. During that month, Roosevelt had reneged on a promise he had given Churchill at Quebec to provide Stage II of Lend-Lease, and he had tried to blackmail Churchill into granting U.S. commercial airlines landing rights on British airfields. Circumstantial evidence strongly suggests that at an off-the-record White House meeting on November 17, Roosevelt had given Admiral King and Secretary of the Navy Forrestal secret instructions that the U.S. Navy should not supply any British military operations against communist-controlled guerrilla forces in Greece.

At best, Roosevelt's treatment of Churchill was oddly inconsistent. At worst, it was more than slightly devious. Nevertheless, any fair judgment of Franklin Roosevelt must be tempered by the reality of his failing health. His vitality, his power of concentration and his clarity of thought were all waning. If he betrayed Churchill over Greece, his memory and his judgment had betrayed him.

CHAPTER SIX

The Sacrifice of Stilwell

*"More than any other American theater commander in the war, Stilwell
required the constant and vigorous political support of his own government,
and less than any other commander did he get it."*

HENRY L. STIMSON
Secretary of War

Joseph Warren Stilwell was born on March 19, 1883, the year after Franklin
Roosevelt's birth. Like the Roosevelts, the Stilwells were an old-line American family. Joseph was the direct descendant of Nicholas Stilwell, who had come to North
America from England in 1638. Joe's father, Benjamin Stilwell, a prosperous businessman with both a medical and a law degree, believed his eldest son needed the
discipline of a military education. Through President William McKinley, young
Stilwell received an appointment to the United States Military Academy at West
Point. There he excelled in French language studies and in sports. Stilwell graduated from West Point in 1904, the same year that his future commander-in-chief graduated from Harvard. The newly commissioned second lieutenant was "a straight,

taut figure of five-foot-nine weighing 145 pounds, with neat head and features, cropped hair, a straightforward look and serious dark eyes."[1]

It is not likely that Stilwell and Roosevelt would have ever met except for two fortuitous circumstances. As a result of military service in China, where he eventually became the U.S. Army attaché at the American Embassy in Nanking, Stilwell acquired a fluency in Chinese and an extensive knowledge of Chinese history, geography and that nation's military strengths and weaknesses. The other circumstance derived from his relationship with a future chief of staff of the U.S. Army, George C. Marshall. Their friendship had been forged in 1926 in Tientsin in north China when they had served together in the 15th Infantry. Three years later, when Marshall was the assistant commandant of the Infantry School at Fort Benning, Georgia, he had made out Stilwell's efficiency report. In answer to the question, what is the highest command Stilwell could be recommended to hold, Marshall wrote, "qualified for any command in peace or war."[2] In early 1942, Marshall was instrumental in Stilwell's selection to be chief of staff to Generalissimo Chiang Kai-shek, the autocratic ruler of China whose country had been at war with Japan for over four years before the attack on Pearl Harbor.

For the first six months of the war in the Pacific, America and her allies experienced one disaster after another. The United States Navy suffered its most humiliating defeat at Pearl Harbor. In the Philippines, most of the Army Air Force was destroyed on the ground. In less than a month, the Army was forced to withdraw into the Bataan Peninsula and the island fortress of Corregidor. The British Crown Colony of Hong Kong surrendered on Christmas Day. In two months, the Japanese drove the British out of Malaya. On February 15, Singapore surrendered. Churchill considered it the greatest disaster in the history of British arms.

Six days after the fall of Singapore, General Sir Archibald Wavell, supreme commander of the newly created theater of operations known as A.B.D.A, (Americans, British, Dutch and Australians) cabled Churchill from his headquarters on the outskirts of Bandoeng in Java, "I am afraid that the defense of A.B.D.A. area has broken down and that defense of Java cannot now last long."[3]

Washington and London were already prepared to write off the Netherlands East Indies. The Dutch capitulated on March 9. The Japanese thrust suddenly turned to the west toward Burma. While Burma contained important natural resources, including oil and timber, Japan's real strategic objectives were to sever the

Burma Road, which went north 350 miles from Rangoon on the coast to the Chinese city of Kunming in Yunnan Province, and to provide a buffer for their recent conquests of Malaya and the Dutch East Indies. The severance of the Burma Road would make it unlikely that America could provide enough of the necessities of war to stave off the collapse of the Chinese army.

Shortly before Stilwell's selection as chief of staff to Chiang Kai-shek, General Marshall had asked Secretary of War Henry L. Stimson to talk to him. They met at the secretary's eighteenth-century home overlooking Rock Creek Park. In front of an open fire, Stimson and Stilwell had a long talk about China. Stilwell gave Stimson his personal assessment of Chiang. He told the secretary that the United States was dealing with an ignorant, suspicious, feudal autocrat who had a deep, but misconceived devotion to China and his role as its savior. When Stimson expressed concern about the inherent difficulties of this assignment, Stilwell assured the secretary that he would go wherever Marshall and Stimson wanted him to go. It was the beginning of a lasting friendship between the secretary of war and the general. Stimson soon became one of Stilwell's greatest admirers.

Chiang Kai-shek's photograph had appeared frequently in American newspapers and magazines. With his clean-shaven skull, his thin ferret-like face, his immaculate uniforms and his overly rigid posture, Chiang stood out. Few failed to recognize him. For many Americans, Chiang was the symbol of a free China heroically resisting the odious Japanese. The questions of what sort of a man Chiang really was, what his vision for China was and how the answers to these two questions might affect Sino-American relations were all too easily deferred. In early 1942, and for over two years thereafter, the only thing that seemed to matter was to keep China in the war. To that end, President Roosevelt was inclined to accommodate Chiang whenever possible.

A few days after the fireside chat, Stilwell told Stimson that it might be well for him to carry a personal message from the president to the generalissimo. The secretary promptly arranged the appointment. On February 8, Stilwell had his first private meeting with the president. During their twenty minutes together, Roosevelt dominated the conversation with a monologue on the war. Finally, Stilwell broke into the president's discourse to ask whether he had a message for Chiang Kai-shek. After some hesitation, the president said, "Tell him we are in this thing for keeps, and we intend to keep at it until China gets back *ALL* her lost territory."[4]

Later that day, Stilwell returned to the White House to meet with Harry Hopkins, of whom Stilwell wrote in his diary, "He had on an old red sweater and crossroads-store shoes, and no garters, and his hair hadn't been cut for eight weeks. I'll forgive him for that if he'll help us out."[5] Hopkins wished Stilwell luck and promised to help. He also made a strangely ironic prediction, telling Stilwell, "You are going to command troops, I believe. In fact, I shouldn't be surprised if Chiang Kai-shek offered you the command of the Chinese Army."[6]

On March 4, Stilwell flew into a remote airfield in northern Burma outside Lashio. There he unexpectedly encountered Generalissimo Chiang Kai-shek, who was making a personal assessment of the Burma situation. Chiang was too busy to have more than a brief discussion with Stilwell, who immediately flew on to Chungking. Shortly afterward, Chiang returned to his capital, where the two men and their staffs held a series of meetings that lasted a week. Stilwell wanted clear-cut authority to command the Chinese forces in Burma, which would soon face an elite Japanese division. On March 11, Stilwell left Chungking for the battle front. Before he departed, the generalissimo assured him, "This morning I have issued orders to place the Fifth and Sixth Armies under your command."[7]

By the time Stilwell reached his first field headquarters at Maymyo, near Mandalay in central Burma, the situation was already ominous. The Chinese were dependent on the British for rice, gas, transport and maintenance. Before the evacuation of Rangoon, the British had stockpiled large quantities of supplies at Mandalay; however, when these were depleted there was no way of replenishing them. Railroads and highways between India and Burma were nonexistent. Another critical problem was lack of air power. For the first three months of the war, the RAF and the AVG, the volunteer group of American pilots under the command of Major General Claire Chennault, had taken a heavy toll of Japanese planes; however, the British Hurricanes and the American P-40s were wasting assets. The Japanese replaced their own losses and gradually gained air superiority. On March 21 and 22, two devastating air raids on the RAF-AVG airfield at Magwe effectively ended Allied air operations in Burma.

After the loss of Rangoon and southern Burma, the British and the Chinese attempted to hold the Japanese south of Mandalay. The British forces known as Burma Corps consisted of the 1st Burma Division and the 17th Indian Division plus the 7th Armored Brigade, "a tough, battle-tried formation from the Middle

East."[8] Burma Corps was under the command of Major General William Slim, heretofore an unknown divisional commander in Iraq. Stilwell commanded seven divisions called the Fifth and Sixth Chinese Armies; however, each division was only one-third the size of a British or Indian division. The supreme Allied commander in Burma was General Sir Harold Alexander. Slim, who became one of the great generals of the Second World War, had reached Burma a few days before Stilwell. Although Stilwell never overcame his prejudice against the British, whom he invariably referred to as "Limeys," he and Slim worked well together most of the time.

At first Chiang would not allow his forces to serve under Alexander, instructing Stilwell merely to cooperate with the British. After Alexander made a quick visit to Chungking, Chiang reluctantly agreed to a unified command. Before the campaign was over, Stilwell learned that the command structure was more difficult than he had imagined. His Chinese division commanders frequently received secret orders from Chiang countermanding his own orders.

Slim understood Stilwell better than most. He later wrote of him:

> He already had something of a reputation for shortness of temper and for distrust of most of the rest of the world. I must admit he surprised me a little when, at our first meeting, he said, "Well, General, I must tell you that my motto in all dealings is 'buyer beware,' " but he never, as far as I was concerned, lived up to that old horse trader's motto. He was over sixty, but he was tough, mentally and physically; he could be as obstinate as a whole team of mules; he could be, and frequently was, downright rude to people whom, often for no very good reason, he did not like. But when he said he would do a thing, he did it. True, you had to get him to *say* that he would, quite clearly and definitely—and that was not always easy—but once he had, you knew he would keep his word. . . . He had a habit, which I found very disarming, of arguing most tenaciously against some proposal and then suddenly looking at you over the top of his glasses with the shadow of a grin, and saying, "Now tell me what you want me to do and I'll do it." . . . Americans, whether they liked him or not—and he had more enemies among Americans than among British—were all scared of him. He had courage to an extent few people have, and determination which, as he usually concentrated it along narrow lines, had a dynamic force. He was not a great

soldier in the highest sense, but he was a real leader in the field; no one else I know could have made his Chinese do what they did. He was, undoubtedly, the most colorful character in Southeast Asia—and I liked him.[9]

Within seven weeks of the fall of Rangoon, the Japanese were able to move the equivalent of three additional divisions by sea to Burma. Siam, which had declared war against the Allies, sent two of its divisions into northeast Burma. In their conquest of Burma, the Japanese army waged war with the single-minded objective of destroying the British and Chinese forces that stood in their way. Their most successful tactic was "the hook," which involved circling behind a British or Chinese unit in order to place a block on their main supply line. Most often this caused the defenders to withdraw troops to reopen the road, following which the Japanese would overrun the forward positions.

Their most hideous tactic was the slaughter, and sometimes torture, of prisoners of war. The British troops regarded the Japanese with a mixture of loathing, fear and respect. The Chinese, who seldom had defeated the Japanese, feared them even more. By April 21, the Chinese Sixth Army had virtually disintegrated; however, in a few minor battles the Chinese and the British units had prevailed. One counterattack personally led by Stilwell is best told by Slim.

> Stilwell, at last having received something approaching accurate information of the Sixth Army debacle, had recalled the 200th Division for a desperate attempt to retrieve the situation. When they drove the Chinese out of Loilem, the Japanese had also occupied Taunggyi, only sixty miles from Thazi, which, if they seized that, too, would cut off the whole of the Chinese Fifth Army. Stilwell himself leading the 200th Division and a regiment of the 2nd retook Taunggyi on April 24. Pushing eastward, he drove the enemy out of Hopong, killing some five hundred, and occupied Loilem. It was a magnificent achievement, made possible only by Stilwell's personal leadership with the very front units . . .[10]

On the evening of April 25, tanks of the 7th Armored Brigade surprised and partially destroyed a Japanese mechanized column advancing toward Meiktila. That same day, however, Alexander, Slim and Stilwell, at a hastily called meeting north of

Meiktila, decided that a general retreat into north Burma was the only means of avoiding a total disaster. It was the beginning of the end in Burma.

Stilwell did not accept defeat easily. He was extremely angry. There was more than a little justification for his anger at Generalissimo Chiang Kai-shek, who sent him a steady stream of orders, some of which were so unrealistic that they bordered on the fantastic. On April 30, Chiang sent Stilwell a radio message to hold Mandalay. He might as well have told him to retake Rangoon.

At least once, Stilwell directed his wrath at Slim. Stilwell had been promised that Slim's 17th Division and 7th Armored Brigade would form the rear guard for the Chinese Fifth Army. When Stilwell received a report that these British units were retreating ahead of the Chinese, he became infuriated and without verifying the accuracy of the report, he sent Slim a message in emotional terms, accusing him of failing to carry out his duty as rear guard. Slim, whose troops were then fighting hard to the south of the Chinese, promptly refuted this charge. A few days later, Stilwell sent a message withdrawing the accusation, which was as close as he could come to an apology.

Stilwell and Slim had reason to be disgusted with the Chinese Fifth Army from its commanding officer on down. Slim has described the retreat of this Army with, perhaps, a degree of understatement.

> While Burma Corps had been thus laboriously and perilously making its way back to India, the remnants of Fifth Chinese Army, covered by Sun's 38th Division, fell back from Shwebo to the north. Fifth Army Headquarters with parts of the 22nd and 96th Divisions, after great hardship, eventually staggered out through the Hukawng Valley. Their conduct on this terrible retreat was, perhaps understandably, not such as to endear them to either local inhabitants or fellow fugitives. They seized trains, ejecting our wounded and refugees, women and children, took all supplies on evacuation routes, and looted villages. Their necessities knew no law and little mercy.[11]

By May 1, it was finally clear to Stilwell that it was time to get out of Burma. He arranged for the bulk of his staff to be flown out of a tiny airstrip at Shwebo fifty miles north of Mandalay. Late that day, a twin engine C-47 landed at Shwebo.

Its pilot and co-pilot were Colonels Caleb Haynes and Robert Scott, commander and executive officer at the new India-Burma-China Ferry Command. They had received an urgent message from General "Hap" Arnold, commander of the U.S. Army Air Force, ordering them to rescue Stilwell. Stilwell refused to fly out of Burma. He gave no reasons to the astonished airmen. Perhaps he did not want to leave the Burmese nurses in his party to the tender mercies of the Japanese army. Perhaps he just wanted to prove how tough he was. In any event, his march out of Burma would become a legend.

Stilwell's party of about one hundred included eighteen American officers, six enlisted men, two doctors, nineteen Burmese nurses, ten Chinese guards, fifteen British commandos and an assortment of cooks, porters, missionaries and civilian refugees. By motor vehicle, they reached Indaw on May 5. The next day they abandoned their trucks and headed into the jungle toward Imphal in Manipur, 140 miles to the west. Their plan called for them to go by trail to the Uyu River, a tributary of the Chindwin, then by raft to its confluence. Afterward, they would have to cross a spur of the Himalayas before descending into the Imphal Valley. Stilwell's most immediate problem was whether their food supply would last. He reckoned that they would have to make fourteen miles a day; otherwise they would run out of food. Wearing his broad-brimmed World War I campaign hat, he led the column at the regulation Army rate of 105 steps a minute. Although he was thirty years older than most of the others, Stilwell never made concessions to his age. Throughout the march, he insisted on ironclad discipline. They were beset by heat, downpours, insects, malaria, dysentery and a rogue elephant. In the first part of their march, there was a possibility that a Japanese patrol would appear out of nowhere. Later, there was a possibility of hostile encounters with armed natives. Neither risk materialized. When Stilwell and his column reached the safety of Imphal on May 20, not a single life had been lost. Slim later wrote of Stilwell's trek, "It was a grueling march and the party owed its survival to the astringent encouragement of the elderly general himself, who proved the stoutest-hearted and toughest of the lot."[12]

Four days after reaching Imphal, Stilwell flew to Delhi, where newspapermen followed him from the airport to the Imperial Hotel. There he agreed to hold a press conference. His concluding words reflected his single-minded determination: "I claim we got a hell of a beating. We got run out of Burma and it is humiliating as hell. I think we ought to find out what caused it, go back and retake it."[13] His words resonated with the American people. They admired his honesty, his lack of pretense and his fighting spirit. They liked the flint-like quality of his character. At a time of defeat "Vinegar Joe" Stilwell became an American hero.

Stilwell had his own strategy for defeating Japan. His first objective was to reopen a land route to China. He preferred to do so through Rangoon, but if that was not feasible, he would build a new road through the jungles of north Burma. His final objective was to lead a combined Chinese-American Army against the large Japanese Army in China.

Stilwell's strategy was based on two questionable assumptions. The first assumption was that the CBI Theater would receive adequate support in troops and logistics when other theaters were considered vastly more important by Marshall and the other members of the joint chiefs of staff. The second was that his strategy would meet with the approval of the British War Cabinet, which under Churchill's leadership considered China a virtually worthless ally.

Stilwell's chances of leading any Chinese Army or combined Chinese-American Army also hinged on his personal relationship with Generalissimo Chiang Kai-shek. By the end of 1942, Stilwell's feelings toward Chiang contained more than a small element of distrust. Chiang had repeatedly ordered his generals to disobey Stilwell whenever he considered the latter's plans carried the risk of too many casualties or too much loss of equipment. Stilwell was convinced that Chiang was conserving his assets for a final showdown with the communist forces after Japan's defeat. He never hid his disdain for Chiang from his staff. His private name for Chiang was "Peanut." He never meant it as a term of endearment.

During the latter part of 1942 and most of 1943, Stilwell devoted all of his energy to the task of creating an independent Chinese force in Ramgarh, India. General Slim, who was nearby training a much larger Anglo-Indian Army, described Stilwell's progress:

> . . . Stilwell, indomitable as ever, planned to raise on this nucleus [Chinese troops who had retreated out of Burma] a strong, well-equipped Chinese force of several divisions that would re-enter northern Burma and open a road to China . . . Stilwell was magnificent. He forced Chiang Kai-shek to provide the men; he persuaded India to accept a large Chinese force, and the British to

pay for it, accommodate, feed and cloth it. The American "Ferry Command" then flew thirteen thousand Chinese from Kunming over the "Hump," the great mountain range between Assam and China, to airfields in the Brahmaputra Valley, whence they came by rail to Ramgarh. This was the first large-scale troop movement by air in the theatre and was an outstanding achievement . . . The two Chinese divisions were reconstituted. Good food, medical care, and regular pay achieved wonders. I have never seen men recover condition as quickly as those Chinese soldiers.[14]

Chiang Kai-shek, however, had scant enthusiasm for Stilwell's achievement. For months the generalissimo had been engaged in a concerted effort to focus Roosevelt's attention on General Claire Chennault and his fledgling Fourteenth Air Force. Chiang had been convinced by Chennault that if sufficient American airpower were based in China, the Fourteenth Air Force could achieve a decisive victory over the Japanese. This would become another way for Chiang to conserve his armies for the future.

Chennault wanted to develop a network of airbases in southeast China from which his planes could attack the Japanese homeland, Japanese shipping in the South China Sea and Japanese military and industrial targets inside China. Stilwell doubted that this strategy would work. Once Chennault's airmen started inflicting serious damage, he believed the Japanese High Command would launch an offensive in east China to overrun the airbases, against which the Chinese army would be ineffective.

In November 1942, Madame Chiang Kai-shek arrived in the United States reportedly for medical treatment. She remained there for over six months. On her arrival at Mitchel Air Force Base in New York on Friday, November 27, she was met by Harry Hopkins. Shortly afterward, Hopkins wrote, "She thinks Stilwell does not understand the Chinese people and that he made a tragic mistake in forcing Chiang Kai-shek to put one of his best divisions in Burma where it was later lost . . . It is pretty clear she does not like Stilwell and expressed the greatest admiration for Chennault."[15]

Toward the end of February, Madame Chiang, who had responded well to her medical treatment, temporarily moved into the White House. Eleanor Roosevelt remembered her guest for her charm and for her "determination that could be as hard as steel."[16] One night at a dinner party, she made a revealing comment about her husband's methods. Eleanor described the scene.

> I had painted for Franklin such a sweet, gentle and pathetic figure that as he came to recognize the other side of the lady, it gave him keen pleasure to tease me about my lack of perception. I remember an incident at a dinner party . . . John Lewis was acting up at the time and Franklin turned to Madame Chiang and asked: "What would you do in China with a labor leader like John Lewis?" She never said a word, but the beautiful small hand came up very quietly and slid across her throat—a most expressive gesture.[17]

Shortly after leaving the White House, she summoned Harry Hopkins, who wrote:

> Mme. Chiang Kai-shek asked me to see her Saturday afternoon and I had a talk of one and a half hours with her. While she said her conversations with the President had gone very well and she believed the conferences she would have with the President tomorrow would satisfactorily complete her talks, I sensed that she was not altogether happy about her visit. She was quite insistent about getting the planes for the new 14th Air Force in there on time and said to me: "We do not want promises that are not fulfilled. The President has told me the planes will get there and he must not let me down with the Generalissimo."[18]

If the president had any lingering doubts about Madame Chiang's advice, they were likely dispelled by his distant cousin Joseph Alsop, an ardent admirer of Chennault, for whom he had served as a staff officer. The relationship between Roosevelt and Alsop was primarily social; however, starting in December 1942, Alsop wrote Harry Hopkins on a regular basis, urging the president to support Chennault. He invariably depicted Stilwell as an "old army" diehard with no comprehension of air power.

Shortly before the Trident conference in May 1943, the president ordered both Stilwell and Chennault back to Washington to make their respective cases.

In an undated diary entry, Stilwell somewhat bitterly revealed that F.D.R had already made up his mind:

> Washington . . . Continual concessions have confirmed Chiang Kai-shek in the opinion that all he needs to do is yell and we'll cave in. As we are doing. FDR had decided on an air effort in China before we reached Washington . . . Nobody was interested in the humdrum work of building a ground force but me. Chennault promised to drive the Japs right out of China in six months, so why not give him the stuff to do it. It was the shortcut to victory.
>
> My point was that China was on the verge of collapse economically. That we could not afford to wait another year . . . That any increased air offensive that stung the Japs enough would bring a strong reaction that would wreck everything and put China out of the war . . .
>
> Henry Stimson and George Marshall were understanding. The War Department was O.K. Even the air was a bit fed up on Chennault. But what's the use when the World's Greatest Strategist is against you?[19]

President Roosevelt's opinion of Stilwell was constantly changing. At times he was inclined to relieve Stilwell, but at other times he backed him completely. One of the latter times was at the first Cairo Conference in November 1943.

On Thanksgiving night, Roosevelt was the host at his villa in Cairo for a traditional dinner for some twenty guests who included Churchill, his daughter Sarah, and Roosevelt's son Elliott, but not Stilwell. The only time the President had for a private talk with Stilwell was after dinner that evening. Around 9:30, Roosevelt asked Hopkins to summon Stilwell. The general's diary reveals nothing of his lengthy conversation with the president, merely stating, "Hopkins sent for me at 9:30. Car lost. Got there at 10:30 band playing—whoopee—talked to Churchill. Hopkins says G-mo [the Generalissimo] as of 6:00 P.M. does not like the plan [for Burma]. My God. He's off again."[20]

Roosevelt's son Elliott kept a record of his father's talk with Stilwell. He later wrote:

... by ten-thirty he and Father were sitting beside each other on the couch in the living room, their heads together. I was sitting some feet away with my brother-in-law John and Harry Hopkins—the three of us talked every now and then, but more often we listened.

"Vinegar Joe" Stilwell talked easily, forthrightly, and quietly. He never raised his voice, and rarely offered any complaints, although it was not difficult to imagine that he would have been justified in doing either or both. A tough row to hoe, that was his lot. He described his difficulties with Chiang and General Ho, Chiang's War Minister, then in answer to a question from Father, he laconically ventured his judgment that he would be able to handle such difficulties . . . It was clear that Father liked General Stilwell: he kept him beside him on the couch for nearly an hour; only then, and with an expression of sympathy from Father on the thorny path he had before him in the East, did he take his leave.[21]

The Cairo Conference weakened Stilwell's plan to recapture north Burma. Chiang and Roosevelt had met in Cairo for the first and last time. Without any prior commitment from Churchill, the president had promised Chiang that, in early 1944, the Allies would invade the Andaman Islands off the Burma coast. Because it would be an all-British operation, Churchill's backing was essential. When Churchill and the British chiefs of staff refused to agree, Roosevelt was forced to notify Chiang that he could not keep his promise. Chiang's first response was to cancel an offensive by his Yunnan army across the Salween River into northeast Burma. This decision directly affected Stilwell, who was counting on the Chinese to divert Japanese forces from his operational area.

Stilwell's principal objective in north Burma was Myitkyina with its strategic airbase. In his drive toward Myitkyina, Stilwell planned to abandon fixed supply lines, to depend on air drops, and to march two hundred miles through jungle, swamp and mountains. All the while he would be opposed by a skillful, entrenched and desperate enemy. Stilwell's two Chinese divisions had been reinforced by a third division flown into India and by an American infantry force designated the 5307th Composite Unit, made up of three battalions. A third of the Americans were combat veterans of the South Pacific. Their code name was Galahad. To the American public, they were always Merrill's Marauders, named after their commanding officer, Brigadier General Frank D. Merrill, a thirty-nine-year-old West Pointer. From

December through mid-March 1944, these units engaged the tenacious Japanese 18th Division, which gradually gave way to Stilwell's forces.

Unknown to Stilwell, the Japanese were poised to launch a major offensive in central Burma. This required substantial reinforcements from areas that the Japanese had conquered earlier in the war. Their 31st Division came from Malaya. Their 54th Division arrived from Java. Their 15th Division marched from Siam. From mid-1943 to January 1944, the Japanese army in Burma rose from four divisions to seven. In addition to their own forces, the Japanese had some 7,000 troops of the Indian National Army under the command of the Indian revolutionary, Subhas Chandra Bose, who believed that India was ripe for a coup. The Japanese also had available the 10,000-man Burma National Army of more dubious quality. From secure airbases in Siam and Malaya, the Japanese moved squadrons of Ki43 fighters to advanced air fields throughout Burma. By January, Japanese fighter aircraft were beginning to show up over central and southern Burma in formations of up to a hundred. The Japanese intended to rely on speed and tactical surprise to defeat the British before they could concentrate their superior forces. The supreme Japanese commander in Burma was Lieutenant General Renya Mutaguchi. He has been described by a British historian as "a fearless ruthlessly ambitious man who reveled in war."[22]

In the second week of March, the Japanese struck. Mutaguchi's primary objective was to surround and then defeat the British forces at Imphal, the capital of Manipur, where he expected to capture food and fuel for his 15th Army, which he could not easily resupply from depots east of the Chindwin River. If he could capture Imphal, Mutaguchi would inflict a major defeat on the British and he would be in a position to trap Stilwell in the jungles of northwest Burma. This all-out offensive by the Japanese 15th Army from mid-March through June resulted in the most decisive battles ever fought in that theater. The outcome would decide Stilwell's fate and perhaps the fate of China.

In the latter part of March, Stilwell's diary reflected the urgency of the rapidly changing situation.

> March 16 After lunch *bad news from Imphal.* Limeys have windup. Flying in 5th Division from Arakan and looking for more troops. This about ruins everything . . .[23]

> March 18 Japs crossed [Indian border] on 16th at
> Hamolin, Tonhe, and Tanngut. Imphal threatened. This ties a
> can to us and finishes up the glorious 1944 spring campaign.[24]

Two weeks later, it seemed even more doubtful to Stilwell that the British could hold. By March 31, Imphal was surrounded. Stilwell wrote, "Situation at Imphal worse then ever."[25] An even more critical situation was developing sixty miles northwest of Imphal around Kohima on the only road linking Imphal with Dimapur, a vast concentration of storage depots, workshops, hospitals and training facilities. At Kohima, the narrow, winding road traversed a 5,000-foot pass before descending forty miles into Dimapur. Slim, the commanding general of the British Fourteenth Army, initially underestimated the threat to Kohima. He later wrote:

> We were not prepared for so heavy a thrust; Kohima with its
> rather scratch garrison and, what was worse, Dimapur with no
> garrison at all, were in deadly peril. The loss of Kohima we could
> endure, but that of Dimapur, our only base and railhead, would
> have been crippling to an almost fatal degree. It would have
> pushed into the far distance our hopes of relieving Imphal, laid
> bare to the enemy the Brahmaputra Valley with its string of air-
> fields, cut off Stilwell's Ledo Chinese and stopped all supply to
> China. . . . The vital need now was to bring in reinforcements,
> not only to replace the vanished reserve in Imphal but, above all,
> to ensure that Dimapur was held.[26]

This nightmare never happened. Major General Sato, commander of the Japanese 31st Division, blindly obeyed his orders to overcome the British garrison at Kohima, which held out against great odds for thirteen days before being relieved. If Sato had bypassed the garrison and advanced forty miles, the greater prize of Dimapur might well have been his. The swirling battles around Imphal and Kohima could not go on for many months because the Japanese lacked the capability of reinforcing and resupplying their forces.

The Japanese were also on the offensive in China. This offensive was code-named Ichi-go. It would be the last major offensive of the Japanese Army in World War II. In its initial phase in April 1944, the Japanese 12th Army advanced into Hunan Province between the Yangtze and Yellow Rivers. Chiang Kai-shek's forces, estimated at no fewer than thirty-four divisions, simply melted before the advancing Japanese. The main purpose of the offensive was to capture the airfields used by Chennault's Fourteenth Air Force in east China. Its secondary purpose was to secure their lines of communication between northeast China and French Indochina.

In June 1944, General Marshall hardly gave the situation in Burma or China his undivided attention. The invasion of France had begun on June 6. Within ten days, Marshall and the other members of the joint chiefs were in France to observe the great battle developing in Normandy. Marshall, however, could have only been pleased with Stilwell's accomplishments in Burma. On May 7, a column of Merrill's Marauders, after a march of almost one hundred miles through the jungle, had surprised the Japanese at Myitkyina and seized the airfield. If they could hold the airfield, it meant that American planes could fly over the Hump on a shorter route at a lower altitude without risk of running into Japanese fighters. By the time of Marshall's return to Washington in late June, General Slim's Fourteenth Army had decisively defeated the Japanese at Imphal. The Japanese commander, Mutaguchi, had advanced into India with an army of 85,000. By the end of June, his army had suffered 53,000 casualties and was in full retreat toward the Chindwin River. It was the decisive victory in Burma.

If Marshall was gratified by the successes in Burma, he was dismayed by the disasters that threatened in China. He was not so much worried over the probable loss of the American airbases in east China as he was over the possibility that the Chinese army would collapse. Should China fall, the United States would have to liberate that vast land, which was defended by a million-man Japanese Army.

Convinced that China was at grave risk of defeat, certain that an American expeditionary force should not be sent there, Marshall conceived the idea of placing Stilwell in command of all the Chinese field armies. With Stilwell's reluctant consent, he circulated the draft of a proposed cable from Roosevelt to Chiang Kai-shek among the other members of the joint chiefs. Marshall presented it to the president as the unanimous recommendation of the joint chiefs. At the same time, they recommended that Roosevelt make Stilwell a four-star general, of whom there were then only four: Marshall, Eisenhower, MacArthur and Arnold.

On July 6, without consulting anyone other than Marshall, Roosevelt dispatched one of his more undiplomatic communications to a head of state. It contained the following:

> The critical situation which now exists, in my opinion calls for the delegation to one individual of the power to coordinate all Allied military resources in China, including the communist forces. I think I am fully aware of your feelings regarding General Stilwell, nevertheless . . . I know of no other man who has the ability, the force and the determination to offset the disaster which now threatens China and our over-all plans for the conquest of Japan. I am promoting Stilwell to the rank of full General and I recommend for your most urgent consideration that you recall him from Burma and place him directly under you in command of all Chinese and American forces, and that you charge him with full responsibility and authority for the coordination and direction of the operations required to stem the tide of the enemy's advances. I feel that the case of China is so desperate that if radical and properly applied remedies are not immediately effected, our common cause will suffer a disastrous setback . . . I assure you that there is no intent on my part to dictate to you on matters concerning China; however, the future of all Asia is at stake along with the tremendous effort which America has expended in that region. Therefore, I have reason for a profound interest in the matter.[27]

Chiang was stunned by Roosevelt's demand; nevertheless, he did not reject it. Instead, he asked for the appointment of an intermediary who would adjust relations between General Stilwell and himself.

Surprisingly, Marshall recommended Major General Patrick J. Hurley for this role. FDR quickly approved. Hurley's instructions were "to facilitate General Stilwell's exercise of command over the Chinese armies placed under his direction."[28] It was not a propitious choice for such an unconventional assignment. Hurley was accompanied to China by Donald Nelson, lately the chairman of the War Productions Board, who also had an inflated view of his own importance. They arrived in Chungking on September 7. Not surprisingly, Marshall expected Hurley to be loyal to Stilwell in all aspects of this assignment. He would soon have ample reason to be disappointed.

Only two days before Hurley's arrival, the Japanese 11th Army had taken the American airfield at Lingling. Their divisions were now less than one hundred miles from the airbase at Kweilin, the hub of Chennault's operations in east China. Writing in his diary on September 9, Stilwell recognized what was coming. "Disaster approaching at Kweilin, nothing to stop the Japs—about 50,000 demoralized Chinese in the area against nine Jap divisions. Chinese have had no replacements. Jap units are filled up. It's a mess and of course all they think of is what we can give them."[29]

On September 15, a new disagreement between Chiang and Stilwell complicated the already stalled negotiations over Stilwell's appointment as commander of the Chinese field armies. In May, Chiang finally had authorized his Yunnan army to advance into northeast Burma. By September, a critical battle had developed at Lungling, the lynchpin of Japanese defenses. In the midst of the battle, Chiang threatened to pull back his army to China unless Stilwell ordered an all-out advance by his depleted Chinese divisions at Myitkyina, which were technically under the overall command of Lord Louis Mountbatten, Supreme Allied Commander, Southeast Asia Command. If Chiang carried out this threat, the completion of the Ledo Road from India to China through the rugged terrain of northern Burma would be delayed indefinitely. One of Stilwell's main objectives was to open up this new supply route to the Chinese front.

Stilwell was beside himself with anger. On September 15 he wrote:

> Chungking, G-Mo calling for me. Took Hurley down at 12:00; one and a half hours of crap and nonsense. Wants to withdraw from Lungling, the crazy little bastard. So either X [Stilwell's Chinese divisions] attack in one week or he pulls out. Usual cockeyed reasons and idiotic tactical and strategic conceptions. He is impossible.[30]

Stilwell promptly warned Marshall of Chiang's threat. Marshall and the other members of the joint chiefs were then at the Quebec Conference with the president. No high-ranking State Department official was present. Marshall responded with alacrity. He quickly convinced King, Leahy and Arnold that Roosevelt should send Chiang a message renewing the previous demand in more compelling terms that Stilwell be appointed commander-in-chief of all Chinese field armies. Marshall's staff drafted the text of the message. Shortly before his departure from Quebec, Roosevelt approved it without change. This message, dated and dispatched September 16, read in part:

> After reading the last reports of the situation in China, my chiefs of staff and I are convinced that you are faced in the near future with the disaster I have feared . . .
>
> I have urged time and again in recent months that you take drastic action to resist the disaster which has been moving closer to China and to you. Now, when you have not yet placed General Stilwell in command of all forces in China, we are faced with the loss of a critical area in east China with possible catastrophic consequences . . .
>
> Only drastic and immediate action on your part alone can be in time to preserve the fruits of your long years of struggle and the efforts we have been able to make to support you. Otherwise, political and military considerations alike are going to be swallowed in military disaster . . .
>
> I am certain that the only thing you can now do in an attempt to prevent the Jap from achieving his objectives in China is to reinforce your Salween armies immediately and press their offensive, while at once placing General Stilwell in unrestricted command of all your forces. . . . In this message I have expressed my thoughts with complete frankness because it appears plainly evident to all of us here that all your and our efforts to save China are to be lost by further delay.[31]

Roosevelt's message went to Stilwell for translation. Stilwell was instructed to deliver the translated message personally to Chiang. His diary reflects how much he relished this assignment:

> September 19 Mark this day in red on the calendar of life. At long, at very long last, FDR has finally spoken plain words, and plenty of them, with a firecracker in every sentence. "Get busy or else." A hot firecracker. I handed this bundle of paprika to the Peanut and then sank back with a sigh. The harpoon hit the little bugger right in the solar plexus, and went right through him. It was a clean hit, but beyond turning green and losing the power of speech, he did not bat an eye. He just said to me, "I

understand." And sat in silence, jiggling one foot. We are now a
long way from the "tribal chieftain" bawling out. *Two long years
lost,* but at least FDR's eyes have been opened and he has thrown
a good hefty punch. I came home. Pretty sight crossing the river:
lights all on in Chungking.[32]

Chiang was offended by the substance of FDR's message and the manner of its
delivery. He felt it should have been delivered by Hurley, the president's personal
envoy, rather than by Stilwell, his subordinate. Sometime over the next six days,
Chiang decided to run the risk of defying the president. In an aide-memoire delivered to Hurley, he informed Roosevelt that while he was willing to place his armies
under the command of an American, he had lost confidence in Stilwell and demanded that he be recalled.

Marshall rallied to Stilwell's defense. At his instigation, the joint chiefs sent
Roosevelt a draft of a proposed message to Chiang. It made three points: that
Stilwell was more likely to succeed as commander-in-chief of the Chinese armies
than any other American; that the tremendous efforts required to win the war tran-
scended personality differences; that the generalissimo's own prestige was directly
involved because the reaction of the American public would be most unfavorable once
they learned that Stilwell had been recalled at the specific request of the Chinese leader.
The draft concluded with these words: "I urge upon you as strongly as I can that you
immediately reconsider your decision in this matter. I am convinced that the action you
take now will have a great effect on the war and also on future relations between the
United States and China."[33]

It was probably the last opportunity to force Chiang to reconsider. At this
point, Chiang had not yet informed the Central Executive Committee of the
Kuomintang of what he had done. Roosevelt, however, did not heed Marshall's
advice.

A few days afterward, a conversation at a Washington dinner party immeasur-
ably strengthened Chiang's hand. H. H. Kung, the wealthy banker who was married
to Madame Chiang's elder sister, was one of the guests, as was Harry Hopkins.
During the course of the evening, he and Hopkins had a private talk. Shortly afterward, Kung cabled Chungking that Hopkins had said that if Chiang insisted on
Stilwell's recall, Roosevelt would yield to the request in as much as it involved the

right of sovereignty. It was, perhaps, a deliberate indiscretion designed to send a signal to Chiang without Marshall's knowledge. Someone in Chungking informed Hurley, who repeated it to Stilwell. In his diary, Stilwell wrote:

> October 1 Pat [Hurley] in with news of Kung to G-mo. FDR "delighted" that U.S. commander will be appointed, and other point is a matter of sovereignty. FDR proceeds to cut my throat and throw me out. Pat feels very low about it. I don't. They just can't hurt me. I've done my best and stood up for American interests. To hell with them.[34]

Within a few days, Stilwell drafted a memorandum, which he filed with his diary, that revealed his unvarnished opinion of Chiang and his thoughts on his own future in China.

> Chiang Kai-shek is the head of a one party government supported by a Gestapo and a party secret service. He is now organizing an S.S. of 100,000 members . . . (He) will not make an effort to fight seriously. He wants to finish the war coasting, with a big supply of material, so as to perpetuate his regime. He has blocked us for three years and will continue to do so. He has failed to keep his agreements . . . He is responsible for major disasters of the war. Nanking, Lan Fang, Changsha and Hengyang, Kweilin and Liuchow . . . But (he) is the titular head of China and has marked me as *persona non grata*.
> Therefore I cannot operate in the China theater while he is in power—unless it is made clear to him that I was not responsible for the September 19 note, and that the U.S. will pull out unless he will play ball.[35]

In an apparent effort to appease Marshall, Roosevelt cabled Chiang with the suggestion that Stilwell remain in command of the Chinese armies in Burma and Yunnan. Chiang would not compromise. On October 13, Hurley, whose seeming distress over Stilwell's plight was utterly false, delivered the coup de grâce. His secret cable directly to the president read in part:

The Generalissimo reacts favorably to logical persuasion and leadership. You can do business with the Generalissimo. He reacts violently against any form of coercion, squeeze play or ultimatum. Stilwell is incapable of understanding or cooperating with Chiang Kai-shek politically. Stilwell has stated that Chiang Kai-shek never acts until action is forced upon him. On this thesis, Stilwell's every act is a move toward the complete subjugation of Chiang Kai-shek. There is no issue between you and Chiang Kai-shek except Stilwell . . . [36]

A curt announcement made at noon in Washington on October 28 revealed to the world that Stilwell had been relieved of all duties and recalled to Washington. His unenviable duties had encompassed being chief of staff to Chiang Kai-shek, Deputy Supreme Allied Commander in Southeast Asia, commanding general of U.S. Forces in the CBI theater, field commander of the Chinese Army in Burma, chief of the Chinese Training and Combat Command and administrator of Lend-Lease to China. Other than Lt. Gen. Walter C. Short, who was relieved ten days after the Pearl Harbor disaster, Stilwell was the only general officer whom FDR relieved during the entire war.

Shortly thereafter, Clarence Gauss, who had spent the most important years of his life in China, submitted his resignation as the United States ambassador to China. He resigned because he had no influence with Chiang and the president was continually bypassing him with special envoys like Hurley. General Hurley was swiftly nominated to be Gauss' successor. He got the appointment because he wanted it, because he was a favorite of Roosevelt's, because he had ingratiated himself with Chiang and because no one had informed Roosevelt of the almost unanimous opposition from the staff of the Chungking Embassy. Hurley also received some help from an unlikely source. W. Averell Harriman was then the American ambassador to Russia. On November 10, Harriman met with the president and Under Secretary of State Edward Stettinius, who would soon replace the ailing Cordell Hull. Harriman much later wrote of their meeting:

Under Secretary of State Stettinius, who sat in on the early part of this talk with Roosevelt, raised the question of a successor to Ambassador Clarence D. Gauss, who was about to come home from Chungking. Several names were mentioned, including that of Donald Nelson. Harriman told the President that Nelson would be the wrong choice because of his "egotistical approach to every question and his unwillingness to cooperate with other people." (To his own regret just a few months later, Harriman put in an oar for General Hurley because of my [Harriman's] conviction that he was completely loyal to the President in carrying out his missions and had a shrewd Irish skill in negotiations.)[37]

General Marshall, acting on Roosevelt's instructions, kept Stilwell virtually incommunicado from his return to Washington on Thursday, November 2, until after the presidential election on the following Tuesday. Yet Marshall had fought hard to save Stilwell. In doing so he had clearly incurred Roosevelt's displeasure. Shortly before Christmas, Vice President Henry Wallace had a long, private conversation with Roosevelt, who revealed a glimmer of the tension between Marshall and himself. He told Wallace:

> You know, I had a devil of a job with Marshall with regard to Stilwell. I had to say to Marshall, "If Chiang were only Generalissimo, I would not have to recall Stilwell just because Chiang doesn't like him. But you must remember that Chiang is president of China."[38]

Three days after Franklin Roosevelt was elected president for the fourth time, the Japanese captured the American airbase at Kweilin. The next day, they seized the airbase at Liuchow. By the end of November, six American airbases scattered throughout east China had been lost. The old infantryman had been right all along. The dimensions of the Chinese debacle were staggering. Chiang had lost eight provinces, half a million soldiers, 100 million civilians and his last access to the coast. It was an ill omen of the ultimate defeat of Chiang's armies four years later by the Chinese communists.

Once Roosevelt had committed himself and the United States to the bold initiative of placing Stilwell in command of all Chinese field armies, he should have stayed the course. In the final analysis, Chiang could not afford to run the risk of losing the indispensable support that Roosevelt alone could provide. What if Stilwell had led a revitalized Chinese army to victory over the Japanese? A victory over the

Japanese almost certainly would have brought forth new leaders in China who would not have tolerated Chiang for long. With new leadership backed by a powerful army, the Chinese nationalists should have been able to secure control of their entire country.

For months President Roosevelt had resorted to ad hoc measures to deal with the China crisis without consultation with either the State Department or the American ambassador in Chungking. He hardly gave China sufficient time and attention. Henry Stimson, in his famous memoir, *On Active Service in Peace and War*, once wrote, "One man simply could not do it all, and Franklin Roosevelt killed himself trying."[39] With all due respect, Stimson was wrong. Because of his failing health, Roosevelt no longer tried to do it all. In 1944, he was absent from the White House more often and for longer stretches than ever before. If the truth be known, Franklin Roosevelt lacked the strength and stamina to carry out his awesome responsibilities.

After the fall of China to communism, it became an article of faith among a considerable number of Sino-American scholars that there was nothing that Franklin Roosevelt or anyone after him could have done to alter the course of events in Asia. Few scholars have suggested that Roosevelt should have used all of his presidential powers to force Chiang out of office.

One of those few was Theodore H. White. White had arrived in Chungking on April 10, 1939. He was a twenty-three-year-old graduate of Harvard who had set out from his home in Boston the previous fall with a letter from James Bryant Conant, president of Harvard, recommending him to the good graces of the entire world as a Frederick Sheldon Traveling Fellow of the University. A year and a half out of Harvard, White became a special correspondent for *Time* magazine in China. Three years out of Harvard, White was handpicked by Henry R. Luce, founder and editor of *Time-Life* and *Fortune,* to be Far Eastern editor of *Time* based in New York. After Pearl Harbor, White returned to China for over three years as *Time*'s bureau chief and its senior war correspondent on the mainland of Asia.

From his wartime experiences, he produced his first two books, *Thunder Out of China,* which he and his co-author, Annalee Jacoby, published in 1946. Two years later he arranged and edited *The Stilwell Papers.* Over the next thirty years, White published nine more books, including a series on the presidential elections of 1960, 1964, 1968 and 1972. In 1978 he published *In Search of History: A*

Personal Adventure, which is, perhaps, his magnum opus. It is a combination of memoir and history at its best. His conclusions on the conflict between Chiang and Stilwell are a synthesis of his experiences in China at the time of the Stilwell crisis, his interpretation of first-hand information he acquired later, including the *Stilwell Papers,* and much reflection.

Shortly before it was announced in Washington that he was being relieved, Stilwell had summoned White and theater critic Brooks Atkinson of the *New York Times* to his headquarters for a candid farewell. He exhorted them to tell the American people the truth about China, but not just yet. *In Search of History* to a large extent vindicates Stilwell, who would have been pleased by the following passages:

> I had come to China believing (Chiang) a national hero. Then, incident by incident, as I accumulated notes, the hero became to me first an unlovely character, then an evil one.[40]

• • •

> All that summer I had followed the disaster in East China from the combat zone, both from our own air bases and on foot with Chinese infantry. I had come over to Stilwell's view completely by early fall of 1944. . . .[41]

• • •

> . . . Stilwell was the first American to insist that our interests required political elimination of a major foreign chief of state. This policy perplexes me with its arrogance. But paradoxically I knew, in Stilwell's case, that he was absolutely right. It would have been better for China, for America, and for the world had Chiang been removed from China's leadership in time. There might then have been some hope of a Chinese leadership more humane, less hostile, just as effective yet more tolerant than the one that succeeded Chiang.[42]

In reaching his decision to sacrifice Stilwell, Roosevelt had thought primarily of Chinese sovereignty as personified by Chiang Kai-shek. His obsession with Chiang's position as head of state left him purblind to the risk he was taking. By caving in to Chiang, Roosevelt had gambled China's future on this "unlovely character." All too soon, America would feel the whirlwind.

CHAPTER SEVEN

Hull, Roosevelt and the Failure of American Foreign Policy

"It will be understood that I, holding these views, followed only with greatest skepticism and even despair the progress of our further dealings with the Soviet leaders, in 1944 and 1945, over Poland."

GEORGE FROST KENNAN
American diplomat

On August 13, 1943, Churchill was visiting Roosevelt at the president's estate at Hyde Park shortly before the first Quebec Conference. That day he delivered a cover letter to the president with two attachments. Of the first attachment, he wrote, "The first of these two papers is a grim, well-written story, but perhaps a little too well-written. Nevertheless if you have time to read it, it would repay the trouble. I should like to have it back when you have finished with it as we are not circulating it officially in any way."[1]

This report of over 5,000 words came from Sir Owen O'Malley, the British ambassador to Poland. It was addressed to Anthony Eden, the British foreign secretary under the date of May 23, 1943. The subject of this paper was "the Katyn Forest

Massacre." For over three years, the Polish government-in-exile, based in London and recognized by both Great Britain and the United States, had been concerned about the fate of over 15,000 Polish officers who were among the 180,000 soldiers and civilian officials taken prisoner by Soviet forces after the Soviet invasion of eastern Poland on September 17, 1939. Ironically, it was Nazi Germany that uncovered this crime. On April 13, 1943, the German wireless publicly disclosed that it had located mass graves containing the remains of the missing Polish officers in a forest near Katyn in eastern Poland. Three days later, the Polish Cabinet in London issued a statement that the International Red Cross in Switzerland had been approached about making an impartial investigation at the site of the mass graves. Subsequently, the British convinced the Polish government to withdraw the request. With great indignation, the Soviet government broke off diplomatic relations with the Polish government, contending that it had acted in collusion with the Germans, who were the perpetrators of this horrific crime.

The Russians gained control of the Katyn area in September 1943, and thereafter a committee composed exclusively of Russians was appointed to investigate the massacre. Their final report, which was issued in January 1944, concluded that the POW camps housing the Polish officers were overrun by German forces in July 1941, after which they were all executed by the SS. Winston Churchill held private doubts about Soviet innocence. On January 30, 1944, he sent Eden the following minute: "I think Sir Owen O'Malley should be asked very secretly to express his opinion of the Katyn Wood inquiry . . ."[2]

O'Malley's original report, written almost fifty years before the Russian government admitted guilt, is still compelling reading.

> We do not know for certain who murdered a lot of Polish officers in the forest of Katyn in April and May 1940, but this at least is already clear, that it was the scene of terrible events which will live long in the memory of the Polish nation . . . positive indications of what subsequently happened to the 10,000 officers there was [sic] none until the grave at Katyn was opened. There is now available a good deal of negative evidence, the cumulative effect of which is to throw serious doubt on Russian disclaimers of responsibility for the massacre. In the first place there is evidence to be derived from the prisoners' correspondence, in respect to which information has been fur-

nished by officers' families in Poland, by officers now with the
Polish army in the Middle East, and by the Polish Red Cross
Society. Up till the end of March, 1940, large numbers of letters had been dispatched, which were later received by the rela-
tives from the officers confined at Kozielsk, Starobielsk and
Ostashkov; whereas no letters from any of them (except from
the 400 moved to Griazovtez) have been received by anybody
which had been dispatched subsequent to that date. The
Germans overran Smolensk [near Katyn] in July, 1941, and
there is no easy answer to the question why, if any of the 10,000
had been alive between the end of May, 1940 and July, 1941,
none of them ever succeeded in getting any word through to
their families . . . In general we have been obliged to deflect
attention from possibilities which in the ordinary affairs of life
would cry to high heaven for elucidation, and to withhold the
full measure of solicitude which, in other circumstances, would
be shown to acquaintances situated as a large number of Poles
now are. We have in fact perforce used the good name of
England like the murderers used the little conifers to cover up a
massacre; and in view of the immense importance of an appearance of Allied unity and of the heroic resistance of Russia to
Germany, few will think that any other course would have been
wise or right . . . At first sight it seems that nothing less appro-
priate to a political dispatch than a discourse upon morals can
be imagined, but yet, as we look at the changing nature of the
international world of today, it seems that morals and international politics are becoming more and more closely involved
with each other. . . . If, then, morals have become involved with
international politics, if it be the case that a monstrous crime
has been committed by a foreign government—albeit a friendly one—and that we, for however valid reasons, have been
obliged to behave as if the deed was not theirs, may it not be
that we now stand in danger of bemusing not only others but
ourselves; of falling, as Mr. Winant said recently at
Birmingham, under St. Paul's curse on those who can see cruel-
ty "and burn not"?[3]

Sir Owen O'Malley's report deserved better than the treatment Roosevelt gave
it. Surely, the president must have read it with repugnance and even horror, but he
apparently failed to convey its substance to either Cordell Hull, his secretary of state,
or to W. Averell Harriman, whom he would soon appoint as his ambassador to

Russia. As recently as 1975, Harriman was still inclined to believe that the Poles had been murdered by the Germans. That year he wrote, ". . . the methodical horror of the deed seemed to stamp it as more German than Russian, even if the evidence of the time was still confused and contradictory."[4] Indeed, the Katyn Forest Massacre was so horrific that if Cordell Hull had known that it was carried out by the NKVD acting on Stalin's orders, the secretary would have had a much more realistic view of Stalin and Soviet aims than the one that he would soon acquire.

In 1943, a long conflict at the highest level of the State Department came to a head. The conflict was between Cordell Hull, the secretary of state and Sumner Welles, the under secretary of state. Their background, education and government service could not have been more different.

Cordell Hull was born in a log cabin on October 2, 1871, in Overton County, Tennessee, on the ridge between the Wolf and Obed Rivers among the foothills of the Cumberland Mountains. His father, William Hull, who was then thirty-one, earned a meager living as a farmer. Gradually, the financial circumstances of the Hull family improved after Cordell's father acquired a better farm and supplemented his income by logging. At the age of sixteen, Cordell made his first trip to Nashville as a raft hand on his father's log raft. His journey took him down the Obed River to its confluence with the Cumberland, then downstream on the latter river to the state capital, a total distance of 220 miles. Over five decades later, Cordell Hull would explain to Stalin how he had helped his father construct rafts by binding logs with hickory walings.

In 1888, his family sent Cordell and his brother, Ress, to far-off Lebanon, Ohio, to attend the National Normal University. Because of his ardor for the law, which had previously inspired him to read Blackstone, Cordell Hull never completed his studies at the National Normal University. During the winter of 1889–1890, Hull read law in the office of Pitts and Meeks in Nashville. In early January 1891, he entered the senior class of the Cumberland Law School in Lebanon, Tennessee, which was then considered one of the greatest second-category law schools in the country. In June 1891, Hull received his law degree from Cumberland before his twentieth birthday.

During the next sixteen years of his life, Hull practiced law, served in the Tennessee legislature and at the age of thirty-one was appointed the presiding judge of the fifth judicial circuit, which required him to hold a week-long term of court every four months in each of the ten counties within the fifth circuit. Through his work as a circuit judge, Hull gained the respect of numerous lawyers and court followers, many of whom helped him in his successful bid for Congress in 1906.

Hull, after serving eleven terms in the House, was elected a Senator from Tennessee in 1931. In both chambers of Congress he was widely respected. Roosevelt appointed Hull secretary of state on the day of his inauguration, March 4, 1933. Hull's prestige in Congress was a large factor in Roosevelt's decision.

Sumner Welles, twenty-one years younger than Hull, came from a wealthy, privileged background. His family sent him to one of New England's most prestigious schools, Groton School in Groton, Massachusetts, which was founded in 1884 by Endicott Peabody on the model of the English public schools. After six years at Groton, he entered Harvard, where he received an A.B. degree in 1914. Franklin Roosevelt had preceded Welles at both Groton and Harvard, which explains in part their easy relationship later in life.

In the 1930s and 1940s, Welles was a familiar presence among social circles in Washington and New York. In Washington, he belonged to the Metropolitan Club and the Riding and Hunt Club, and in New York to the Knickerbocker Club and the Union Club. He frequently carried a Malacca cane on his walks from the old State Department to the Metropolitan Club. In the sweltering Washington summers, he invariably wore an impeccable Panama.

Welles was, however, much more than a dapper, well-dressed diplomat. He was a formidable presence in the State Department and at the White House. He had entered the Foreign Service shortly after his graduation from Harvard. Within a little over a decade, his reputation as an expert on foreign policy was such that when Franklin Roosevelt was governor of New York he had called on Welles for assistance in drafting an article for the highly regarded publication *Foreign Affairs*.

On May 21, 1937, President Roosevelt appointed Welles under secretary of state despite Hull's well-known dislike for the much younger man. The secretary of state and the under secretary of state occupied adjoining offices, but this was the only way the two were close. Their relationship steadily deteriorated. In early 1940, Roosevelt selected Welles to be his special representative to report on conditions in war-torn Europe. It has been described as an "impulsive decision."[5] Roosevelt had hoped that Welles' mission would delay the German offensive in the West. In the event, Welles visited the capitals of Great Britain, France, Italy and

Germany, where he conferred with Chamberlain, Daladier, Mussolini and Hitler. Nothing of substance was accomplished, but the mission did serve as a pointed reminder to Hull of Welles' high standing with the president. In August of the following year, Welles again upstaged Hull. The president invited Welles to his historic conference with Churchill at Placentia Bay off the coast of Newfoundland. Hull had been excluded. Furthermore, Roosevelt had kept his entire Cabinet in the dark about the planned conference.

By August 1943, the animosity between Hull and Welles was adversely affecting the State Department. Dean Acheson wrote:

> Increasingly Welles worked directly with the president, naturally enough in view of their close relationship and of Welles' incisive mind and decisive nature. He grasped ideas quickly and got things done. More and more he took over liaison with the White House on international political matters. Mr. Hull rankled under what he believed to be Welles' disloyalty and the president's neglect. The Department became divided into Welles men, who looked to the under secretary, particularly in the Latin American field, and Hull men, who sought guidance from the chief. This unhealthy situation blew up in August, 1943, when as Mr. Hull relates it, he asked the president to remove Welles and the president complied. Meanwhile it poisoned the Department.[6]

In his memoir, Cordell Hull contended that the principal reasons that the president removed Welles as under secretary were his inclination to make speeches on postwar foreign policy without the secretary's prior approval, and his habit of going over Hull's head directly to the president. While this explanation has considerable truth, it evades the real issue with which Roosevelt had been confronted. Hull had shown Roosevelt affidavits stating that Welles, who was married, had been involved in homosexual behavior. Hull insisted that because of the risk of blackmail and the need to spare the State Department from an extremely messy scandal, the president had to ask for Welles' resignation. Roosevelt, who already had learned of the problem from other sources, reluctantly agreed. At the end of August, Welles resigned at the president's request.

In the following weeks, Roosevelt sought to soften the blow to Welles by finding a prestigious diplomatic assignment for him. When Stalin insisted that the prerequisite to a summit meeting with Roosevelt and Churchill was a meeting of the foreign ministers of Russia, the United States and Great Britain in Moscow, Hull told the president that he was too old and too ill to undertake such a long and arduous assignment. The president initially approached his new ambassador to Russia, W. Averell Harriman, about standing in for Hull. Harriman told the president that, inasmuch as the Russians were impressed by rank, if Cordell Hull could not go, then the chief of the U.S. delegation should be Sumner Welles. The president immediately concurred. When he called Welles at Bar Harbor, Maine, Welles was unenthusiastic. The president gave him time to think about it. Meanwhile, Cordell Hull got wind of what was happening. He erupted with fury over the prospect of Welles taking his place. Notwithstanding his previous statements about his age and his health, he insisted that as secretary of state he had the right to attend this conference of foreign ministers as the chief representative of the United States. The president acquiesced.

Hull arrived in Moscow late in the afternoon of October 18, 1943, in a new C-54 transport plane. Hull and his entourage, which included Ambassador Harriman and his daughter, Kathleen, got off the plane in biting cold. They were greeted by four high-ranking officials including V. M. Molotov, the Russian foreign minister. Hull had gone to Moscow with the strong conviction that the most important thing he could accomplish was a four-power declaration agreeing to continue wartime cooperation into the postwar era and to form a new international organization to maintain world peace. Hull did succeed in getting such a declaration. Although the Chinese foreign minister had not been invited to the conference, Hull, with some difficulty, had convinced the Russians to allow the Chinese to be a signatory.

Throughout Hull's more than two weeks in Moscow, both Molotov and Stalin treated the elderly secretary of state with great courtesy. It was a shrewd stratagem that would pay handsome dividends. On the evening of his arrival, Hull met with the other two foreign ministers at the Kremlin. He described the atmosphere of this initial meeting as one "with every appearance of cordiality and cooperation and a strict attendance to business."[7] Hull did not see Stalin until October 25, and then only because he had requested a meeting with the Soviet leader. Hull explained why he had hesitated to request such a meeting. "My theory was that I should do business with Molotov and not let him think I wished to go over his head to Stalin."[8] At their only formal meeting, Hull lavished praise on Molotov and the Soviet government. He would later write, "I told Stalin of my pleasure at being in Moscow, which was in fulfillment of a long-held desire to visit his country. I said I had attended many international conferences in my life, but at none had I received greater hospitality and consideration than we had from our hosts, the Soviet government, and particularly Molotov."[9]

Because of his uncertain health, Hull avoided all social functions in Moscow except for a banquet which Stalin gave on the final night of the conference, October 30. The venue for the banquet was the Catherine the Great Hall of the Kremlin. Hull was seated on Stalin's right. The Soviet leader opened the conversation saying, "You have had a successful conference."[10] Hull "at once replied that the credit was entirely his [Stalin's], that he had authorized his great country to take the decisive step of joining with Great Britain and the United States in a world program based on cooperation."[11] Hull recalled Stalin's reaction. "This seemed to please him. Throughout the conversation, he expressed himself as unqualifiedly for a broad program of international cooperation—military, political, and economic—for peace."[12]

Hull was almost euphoric over Stalin's promises to cooperate with the United States and Great Britain. He apparently sincerely believed that Stalin was a great man who was universally admired. At that moment, he assured Stalin of his high standing among the people of the world and alluded to Stalin's place in history. "I remarked that he had no idea how great was his prestige in the world . . . Real leaders appear in the world only every one or two centuries. You yourself have demonstrated that leadership both at home and abroad . . ."[13]

The last time that Hull would ever see Stalin was around 2:00 A.M. on October 31. Stalin's words and gestures deeply moved him.

> I had an impressive experience with Stalin as we parted. After the usual expression of leave-taking, he shook hands with me and said "Goodbye" in Russian. Then, after walking three or four steps away from me, he suddenly turned and walked back and shook hands a second time to a rather protracted extent, but without saying a word. Then, with serious demeanor, he turned and walked away.[14]

Hull departed Moscow by plane on November 3 in a sanguine mood. He later wrote, "As I boarded the plane for home, I felt very strongly that great things had been accomplished at Moscow."[15] For one who occupied the senior Cabinet post and who was second in succession to the presidency, this was a potentially dangerous delusion. Moreover, Hull was oblivious to his most serious mistake in Moscow. He had failed to engage the Soviets in any serious dialogue over Poland.

In October 1943, the relations between Poland and Russia were going from bad to worse. The most obvious sticking point was Russia's refusal to restore recognition of the Polish government-in-exile. The Poles were more than a little leery of Russia's future intentions. They had learned from reliable sources that Stalin coveted that part of Poland that lies to the east of the Curzon Line even though it had never been recognized as an international boundary. There was almost a universal feeling among Poles that the Soviet forces would not leave after they had driven out the Germans. The leaders of the Polish government-in-exile looked to the United States and Great Britain to protect Poland from any interference in its internal affairs by the Soviet Union.

At the Moscow Conference, at which Poland was unrepresented, Cordell Hull did virtually nothing to advocate any position favorable to the Polish nation. On October 24, Anthony Eden spoke privately to Hull about lining up United States support to put pressure on Molotov to restore diplomatic relations with Poland. After Eden had presented the British position to Molotov in a comprehensive way, Hull merely gave it a lukewarm endorsement, telling Molotov "that when two neighbors fall out, the other neighbors, without going into the causes or merits of the dispute, were entitled to express the hope that these differences could be patched up."[16] The operative words were "without going into the . . . merits of the dispute." Hull's memoir contains the following partial explanation of why he refused to look at the merits of that dispute.

> When I left office, the Polish-Russian dispute was no nearer solution. I have no intention to go into the merits of that dispute. The policy of the President and me was to refrain from stretching the United States upon a bed of nettles. In our diplomatic exchanges with both sides and in our offers of good offices, we repeatedly stated we were not entering into the merits of the differences between Poland and Russia.[17]

One particular issue that Hull wanted to avoid was the location of the postwar border between Poland and Russia. When Molotov refrained from raising the issue, Hull was much relieved. He later wrote, "Russia, moreover, never once raised the question that had disturbed us the previous year, namely, the settlement at this time of postwar frontiers."[18]

Hull's adamant refusal to engage Molotov and Stalin in any meaningful discussions about Poland has never been fully explained. The publication in 1965 of the third and final volume of Anthony Eden's memoirs shed some light. By then Hull was a largely forgotten figure and Eden's reputation had been irreparably damaged by the Suez fiasco of 1956; nevertheless, Eden made a not insignificant contribution to the history of his time by revealing Roosevelt's lack of confidence in Hull as well as the president's proclivity for making foreign policy his private preserve. Eden's memoir contains the following passage:

> But there was one ominous void in our discussions. In recent months the Soviet armies had advanced some two hundred miles on the central and southern sectors of the front. Once they were into Poland, our negotiating power, slender as it was anyway, would amount to very little. With this in mind I had two talks with Mr. Hull, but I found him most unwilling to make any move. He argued that he had no instructions about Poland and that he could not go beyond his authority. This seemed to me unnecessarily reserved, because I was not suggesting detailed discussion about frontiers. The Polish Government had told me they were not ready for this, only that we should show keen concern for Poland's future. But I was unable to shake Mr. Hull.[19]

Hull's thinking about Soviet-American relations, throughout the Moscow Conference and during most of his remaining twelve months as secretary of state, was characterized by excessive optimism. He remained purblind to the risk that Stalin would install a puppet regime in Warsaw that was totally obedient to Moscow. This optimism reached its peak a few days after his return to Washington. Hull's address to a joint session of Congress on November 18, 1943, stands as one of the most visionary and myopic speeches ever delivered by a secretary of state on the foreign policy of the United States. In this address, Hull stated:

> As the provisions of the Four-Nation Declaration are carried into effect, there will no longer be need for spheres of influence, for alliances, for balance of power, or of any other of the special arrangements through which, in the unhappy past, the nations strove to safeguard their security or to promote their interests. . . . I found in Marshal Stalin a remarkable personality, one of the great statesmen and leaders of this age.[20]

President Roosevelt held a similar view of Soviet-American relations. Hull later wrote of this. "President Roosevelt and I saw alike with regard to Russia. We both realized that the path of our relations would not be a carpet of flowers, but we also felt we could work with Russia. There was no difference of opinion between us on the basic premise that we must and could get along with the Soviet government."[21]

Robert Murphy was among a handful of foreign service officers who were far more skeptical about future cooperation with the Soviet Union. His career with the State Department included conventional diplomatic assignments in Switzerland, Germany and France before World War II. After the fall of France in 1940, President Roosevelt summoned him to the White House to discuss a top secret mission to French North Africa. On December 18, 1940, an Air France seaplane touched down in the harbor of Algiers. Murphy was one of the passengers. He spent most of the next two years there, where he had an office at the American consulate general. Acting on secret instructions from President Roosevelt, Murphy cultivated top French military leaders whom he assured that the defeat of Nazi Germany was certain. In private conversations, he adjured them to be on the victorious side. Through these contacts, he was able to ascertain which of the French commanders would cooperate in the event of an American invasion of French North Africa. The president had ordered Murphy to communicate directly with the White House without apprising the State Department of his reports to the president. Consequently, when the Allies commenced their invasion of North Africa on November 8, 1942, Murphy had known about it well in advance, but Secretary of State Hull had not.

Ironically, eleven months later, Murphy was assigned to be Hull's aide when he arrived in North Africa en route to the Foreign Ministers' Conference in Moscow. Murphy's account of Hull's thinking on the eve of the conference is illuminating:

The Allied Advisory Council on Italian and Balkan Affairs . . . was created in Moscow in October, 1943, when the Foreign Ministers of the Big Three—the United States, the Soviet Union and Great Britain—conferred there. The American representative at this meeting was Secretary of State Hull, who insisted on making this arduous wartime journey in person although he was then seventy-two years old, in very poor health, and had never before flown in an airplane. Upon his doctor's advice, Hull traveled the transatlantic portion of his voyage on a cruiser, and I met the warship at Casablanca and rode with the secretary on his plane to Algiers.

I was astonished to discover how emotional Hull was about the conference he was about to attend. He expressed confidence that it would be an epochal event. I had not thought about it in that light, considering it merely a preparatory discussion, but Hull was almost mystical in his approach. The veteran Tennessee politician had become fascinated with the possibilities of establishing close, friendly relations with Soviet Russia. During Hull's eleven years as Secretary of State, his attitude on many matters was misjudged by the Washington press corps, especially his attitude toward Russia. Hull often was depicted as the most anti-Soviet member of the Roosevelt cabinet, whereas he was virtually co-creator with the president of the "Grand Design" for the postwar world, a plan which assumed that the United States and Soviet Russia could become partners in peace because circumstances had made them partners in war.[22]

During the first six months of 1944, both the president and his secretary of state virtually ignored the tensions between Poland and Russia, as well as the potential problems for all of Eastern Europe, which the Red Army would inevitably occupy. In 1944, Roosevelt rarely called on Hull for advice regarding relations with Britain or Russia. It was even more rare for the secretary of state to offer advice to the president on such vital matters; however, circumstances forced him do so on at least two occasions.

In June, Stanislaw Mikolajczyk, the prime minister of Poland, after many months of deliberately stalled negotiations over his visit, had received permission to come to Washington for meetings with the president. Because of the presidential election, Roosevelt had placed stringent conditions on Mikolajczyk's activities. He was prohibited from meeting with any Polish-American groups and from making any political speeches that might stir up anti-Russian feeling.

At his first meeting with Roosevelt, the prime minister "asked him what had been decided about the future Polish frontiers at Teheran."[23] The president replied, "Stalin wasn't eager to talk about it . . . I want you to know that I am still opposed to dividing Poland with this line [the Curzon Line] and that eventually I will act as a mediator in this problem and effect a settlement."[24] Afterward the Polish leader learned the truth about the Teheran Conference. He would write, "I later learned that Roosevelt had only a few months before agreed to turn over to Stalin the huge section of Poland that the Red Army had invaded while an Axis partner. But at this time his manner was one of great courtesy."[25]

The only concrete result of Mikolajczyk's visit to Washington was Roosevelt's action in initiating a meeting between Mikolajczyk and Stalin in Moscow. The prime minister suspected this was largely a spur-of-the-moment suggestion, and that little would be accomplished by going to Moscow. He was right on both counts.

Hull's involvement in Mikolajczyk's nine-day mission to Washington was limited to a twenty-five minute conference on June 12. The next day, Hull prepared a memorandum for the president regarding the possible future interests of the United States in Polish problems. The president never read Hull's memorandum before his final conference with Mikolajczyk.

What Roosevelt expected to accomplish by a meeting between Mikolajczyk and Stalin is unclear. He probably hoped that such a meeting would result in the restoration of diplomatic relations between the two countries; however, Stalin had never given Roosevelt much cause for hope. The Polish prime minister arrived in Moscow late on July 30 and did not leave the Russian capital until August 10. Two days after his arrival, the Polish underground army began its doomed battle for control of Warsaw. Stalin solemnly told Mikolajczyk that he would do his best to help Warsaw; however, on his return to London, Mikolajczyk received a chilling cable from Stalin that read in part, "After a closer study of the matter I have become convinced that the Warsaw action . . . is a thoughtless adventure causing unnecessary losses among the inhabitants. . . . In view of this state of affairs the Soviet Command cuts itself away from the Warsaw adventure and cannot take any responsibility for it."[26] A few days later, Stalin refused permission for American planes to refuel at Russian airfields after they had dropped supplies to the Polish forces in

Warsaw. To his credit, Hull gave the president the following advice: "I believe for a number of considerations that it is impossible for us or the British to abandon to their fate the Polish underground forces which are actively fighting the Nazi invaders of their country simply because such action might not accord with Soviet political aims."[27]

For a few heroic weeks in August 1944, Polish forces had a window of opportunity to liberate Warsaw and to reestablish their own government in their own capital. To make this happen, Roosevelt's support was vital. What was required was an exceptionally bold operation to airlift supplies to Warsaw and his steadfast loyalty to the Polish government in London. In the event, Roosevelt was neither exceptionally bold, nor steadfastly loyal.

On August 24, the president sent messages to both Churchill and Mikolajczyk. His cable of that date to Churchill was bleakly pessimistic:

> My information points to the practical impossibility of our providing supplies to the Warsaw Poles unless we are permitted to land on and take off from Soviet airfields, and the Soviet authorities are at the present time prohibiting their use for the relief of Warsaw.
>
> I do not see that we can take any additional steps at the present time that promise results.[28]

Roosevelt was never willing to support Churchill in putting pressure on Stalin to allow British and the American planes to land on Russian airfields.

On the same date, Roosevelt sent Mikolajczyk in London a letter that raised a new and disturbing issue:

> For your strictly confidential information I am glad to assure you that the United States Government has urged the Soviet Government to cooperate in getting aid to the Polish forces in Warsaw and Mr. Churchill and I have addressed a personal message to Marshal Stalin expressing the hope that he will give immediate orders to drop supplies and munitions to the Polish forces in that city, or that he will agree to help our planes in this task.
>
> I have not given up hope that our intervention will have the desired results.

> In regard to the broader question of the solution of Polish-Soviet differences, I fully realize the difficulties which confront you, particularly in light of the heroic and unequal struggle of the Warsaw garrison. I feel, however, that these unfortunate developments should not deter you from presenting reasonable proposals to the Polish Committee of National Liberation and I am of the firm opinion that if reasonable proposals are not presented to the Committee, and if a crisis should arise in the Polish Government, such developments could only worsen the situation.[29]

The last paragraph of Roosevelt's letter clearly undermined Mikolajczyk. Here was the leader of the world's most powerful democracy urging the prime minister of Poland to reach an accommodation with the Soviet-backed Polish Committee of National Liberation, which had no legitimacy whatsoever to act in any capacity on behalf of the Polish people. Mikolajczyk never forgave Roosevelt for this letter. Three years after the war, with his country in the iron grip of a communist dictatorship, Mikolajczyk wrote of the August 24 letter with some asperity:

> Roosevelt replied to me on August 24. His letter involved much more than the question of air aid and his request for the use of Russian landing strips. The letter marked his acceptance of the Lublin Poles [the Polish Committee of National Liberation] as the bona fide leaders of the nation.[30]

Because of failing health and fatigue, Hull turned down the president's invitation to attend the second Quebec Conference in September. At this point in time, the war was going so well that the president did not foresee any controversies involving military operations, nor did he anticipate any serious negotiations over foreign policy. His invitation to Hull to attend the Quebec Conference seems to have been mainly a matter of courtesy.

With an approaching election, however, FDR knew that Hull could be useful because of his personal prestige with the American people as one of their elder statesmen. On the last Friday in September, he sent Hull a memorandum requesting him to make two speeches on national radio before election day, and also requesting him to draft a foreign policy speech for the president covering the following points:

(1) What we have done in the past to promote peace in the world.
(2) What we have done to promote international trade.
(3) How we tried to keep our own peace after Poland was attacked and before Pearl Harbor.
(4) Some of the specific steps taken by the Republican leaders to block our efforts in all these things.
(5) The steps we have taken for the future peace of the world in the past two years.
(6) The prospects of a permanent international peace in the future.[31]

Even before he received this memorandum, Hull had already made up his mind to call on the president the following Sunday to inform him of his decision to resign. When they met on Sunday, October 1, Hull told Roosevelt, "I had been overexerting myself for some time and now found myself in such physical condition that I should have to resign."[32] He also informed Roosevelt that he was leaving his office within another day or two to go straight to bed, where he would remain for an indefinite period. Hull later wrote, "The President did not seem to want to believe me."[33]

Hull had not exaggerated his medical problems. The next day, on his seventy-third birthday, he left the State Department—never to return.

Throughout 1944, American policy toward Russia and Eastern Europe was feckless. If the president and his secretary of state had sought the advice of one particular foreign service officer, their whole attitude toward Soviet-American relations might well have changed. In the summer of 1944, George Frost Kennan was serving as the minister-counselor of the American embassy in Moscow. At the age of forty, he was already the senior member of the diplomatic corps in Moscow in length of service. Kennan had first arrived in Moscow in December 1934, two months before his thirtieth birthday, as the aide to Ambassador William C. Bullitt. Bullitt had selected Kennan because he spoke Russian and had been able to answer Bullitt's questions about the Russian economy. Kennan had met twice with President Roosevelt on matters of some importance. At their first meeting in 1943, Roosevelt had given Kennan a personal letter to be hand-carried to Dr. Antonio Salazar, the

Portuguese prime minister, giving him the president's pledge that the United States would respect Portuguese sovereignty over the Azores, where the U.S. chiefs of staff wanted to establish airbases. In the spring of 1944, he had met with the president to discuss the boundaries of the Russian zone of occupation after the German surrender. On each occasion, the president had received Kennan graciously.

Before his return to Russia in June, Kennan had felt misgivings about U.S. policy toward Russia, but having been away from that country for seven years he had some uncertainty about the validity of his misgivings. What he saw and experienced in Moscow in the summer of 1944 quickly dispelled any uncertainties. Kennan felt a compelling duty to write a comprehensive essay on the nature of the Soviet leaders and of the situation in which they found themselves as they entered the closing phase of the war for the benefit of his ambassador, W. Averell Harriman, who, he hoped, would make it available to those who had the responsibility for the formulation of American policy.

Kennan's essay was a brilliant analysis of Soviet thinking, Soviet intentions and the man who ruled from the Kremlin. It far surpassed anything like it that had ever emanated from the Moscow embassy. He accurately predicted the course of events in eastern Europe.

> It would be useful to the Western world to realize that despite all the vicissitudes by which Russia has been afflicted since August, 1939, the men in the Kremlin have never abandoned their faith in that program of territorial and political expansion which had once commended itself so strongly to Tsarist diplomatists, and which underlay the German-Russian Nonaggression Pact of 1939. The program meant the re-establishment of Russian power in Finland and the Baltic states, in eastern Poland, in northern Bukovina, and in Bessarabia. It meant a protectorate over western Poland and an access to the sea for the Russian Empire somewhere in East Prussia.[34]

• • •

> For the smaller countries of eastern and central Europe, the issue is not one of communism or capitalism. It is one of the independence of national life or of domination by a big power which

has never shown itself adept at making any permanent compro-
mises with rival power groups.[35]

Kennan knew how difficult it was for the American mind to understand Russia.
He observed:

> It will have to understand that for Russia, at any rate, there
> are no objective criteria of right and wrong. There are not even
> any objective criteria of reality and unreality. What do we mean
> by this? We mean that right and wrong, reality and unreality, are
> determined in Russia not by any God, not by any innate nature
> of things, but simply by men themselves. Here men determine
> what is true and what is false.[36]

Kennan painted a vivid and in many ways perceptive portrait of Stalin; yet he
hesitated to characterize Stalin as irredeemably evil. The wartime alliance required a
certain amount of circumspection. Kennan wrote:

> Joseph Vissarionovich Stalin, now in the sixty-fifth year of
> his life and the twentieth year of his power in Russia, is the most
> powerful and the least known of the world's rulers. . . . There
> are certain points about Stalin which are important to remem-
> ber. First—that he is a Georgian . . . he has not lost the charac-
> teristics of his native environment. Courageous but wary; quick
> to anger and suspicious but patient and persistent in the execu-
> tion of his purposes; capable of acting with great decision or of
> waiting and dissembling, as circumstances may require; out-
> wardly modest and simple, but jealous of the prestige and dig-
> nity of the state which he heads; not learned, yet shrewd and
> pitilessly realistic; exacting in his demands for loyalty, respect,
> and obedience; a keen and unsentimental student of men—he
> can be like a true Georgian hero, a great and good friend or an
> implacable, dangerous enemy. It is difficult for him to be any-
> thing in between.[37]

A few days after completing his essay in September 1944, Kennan
presented it to his chief. Some days later, Harriman returned it without
comment. To this day Kennan does not know whether Harriman read it in full, in

part or not at all. In his book *Special Envoy to Churchill and Stalin 1941–1946,* Harriman never mentions Kennan's essay.

Harriman returned to the United States for consultations in October. Shortly thereafter, he asked FDR for permission to make a radio speech in support of the president's reelection. Roosevelt readily granted permission and on November 3, Harriman spoke on NBC for fifteen minutes. His speech included the statement, "Never in the history of the world has one man—Roosevelt—had the confidence of the peoples of so many nations or of their leaders."[38] It would have been obvious to most of his radio audience that Stalin was the primary leader that Harriman had in mind.

After the election, Harriman had three more talks with Roosevelt during which he had difficulty capturing the president's attention on the unsolved problems in Eastern Europe. At one point, Roosevelt confided, "He wanted to have a lot to say about the settlement in the Pacific, but that he considered the [Eastern] European questions were so impossible that he wanted to stay out of them as far as practicable, except for the problems involving Germany."[39] There is no evidence that Harriman ever gave Roosevelt a copy of Kennan's essay. A wiser man than Harriman would have immediately forwarded it to the president marked "top secret for the president's eyes only."

October was a hard month for Cordell Hull. Neither his health nor his relationship with Roosevelt improved. After spending eighteen days at his Washington apartment vainly trying to regain his health, he entered the Bethesda Naval Hospital where he would remain for almost seven months.

Shortly after Hull entered Bethesda, Vice Admiral Ross T. McIntire unexpectedly appeared in Hull's hospital room. It quickly became apparent to Hull that McIntire was not there merely as a concerned friend. Although McIntire had no responsibility for Hull's care and treatment, he proceeded to give him a prognosis that was almost certainly contrived. He reassured Hull that he would recover sufficiently to resume his duties as secretary of state within a reasonable period of time. McIntire's visit was followed shortly by a visit from the president himself. In his memoir, Hull writes, "Then the president visited me for an hour and a half during which he urged upon me the wisdom of not resigning."[40] This bare statement of fact hardly conveys the dramatics of what transpired. For some obscure reason, Roosevelt put extreme pressure on his ill secretary of state.

Seven months later, when Hull's health was considerably improved, Henry Wallace, then secretary of commerce under President Truman, went to see Hull. The seventy-three-year-old Tennesseean told Wallace, "How he had worked himself completely out and then, when he had gotten so low that he felt he couldn't go along, the President came out to see him to try to persuade him that he shouldn't resign . . . and that he felt like he was practically dead when the argument began and he felt like he was really dead when the argument ended."[41] Wallace's diary indicates that McIntire followed up Roosevelt's visit with a second visit of his own, and spent forty minutes arguing with Hull over why he should not resign. Hull's resolve did not weaken and he tended his written resignation on November 23, to become effective on November 30.

Three days earlier the president informed forty-four-year-old Edward R. Stettinius Jr., who was then under secretary of state, that he had been selected to succeed Hull. Stettinius had been an enthusiastic but mediocre student at the University of Virginia, where he was head cheerleader. He subsequently achieved meteoric success in the corporate world before he was forty. He has been described by Dean Acheson as "enthusiastic, good-natured . . . with prematurely white hair, an engaging smile and a gift for public relations."[42] Charles Bohlen wrote that Stettinius "knew very little history but . . . had shown considerable ability in handling Lend-Lease affairs . . . His mild personality was an asset, too, since it was unlikely that he would cause much trouble. He would not be disposed to disagree with anything Roosevelt or Hopkins wanted to do."[43]

There are curious conflicts in the accounts of Stettinius' appointment. Robert E. Sherwood wrote, "When it was finally decided that Stettinius should be promoted from under secretary to the senior cabinet post there was no doubt in anyone's mind that Hopkins was largely responsible."[44] Sherwood's book was published in 1949. Over twenty-five years later, Averell Harriman's book included extracts from contemporaneous notes concerning Hopkins' advice to FDR on whom he should appoint. "Hopkins said that he was using all his influence to see James F. Byrnes appointed in Hull's place. I heartily endorsed that."[45]

Henry Morgenthau Jr., Roosevelt's secretary of the treasury, kept notes of a conversation with Eleanor Roosevelt on November 27, the same day that the president summoned Stettinius. "I said that I didn't think Stettinius was ideal, but I thought he was the best man I could think of from the President's standpoint as the

President likes to be his own Secretary of State, and what he wanted was merely a good clerk."[46]

Stettinius may have been unaware of the president's aversion to anyone making a record of his private conversations. In any event, shortly after his meeting with the president that day, Stettinius wrote down his recollections. They do not reflect well on either Stettinius or the president. Stettinius quoted Roosevelt as follows:

> . . . I want you to be my secretary of state. I had three under consideration—Henry Wallace, Jimmy Byrnes, and yourself. It would have killed the secretary [Cordell Hull] to have Henry. As for Jimmy, he has no understanding of geography. Of course in the whole foreign situation I am going to have to work awfully intimately with Stalin and Churchill. Jimmy has always been on his own in the Senate and elsewhere and I am not sure that he and I could act harmoniously as a team. . . . You and I could have a perfect understanding and complete harmony and work as a team, you recognizing the big things I would have to handle, at your suggestion.[47]

Stettinius interjected, "In other words, Jimmy might question who was boss."[48] FDR replied, "That's exactly it."[49]

After lunch, their conversation drifted away from affairs of state to Stettinius' plans for his future. "I said I wanted him to know what I was going to do after the war. I said I had the swellest set-up, I would have the presidency of the University of Virginia and Twentieth Century Fox had offered me the chairmanship of the board which would carry $100,000 a year and involve nothing other than attending directors' meetings. He said, 'That's the damnedest thing I ever heard of. My wouldn't it be fun!'"[50]

The president spent most of December at Warm Springs, and at his family estate outside Hyde Park. He and Stettinius met only twice that month. Before their first meeting, Stettinius had learned that a prominent Republican senator was perturbed over developments in Poland. On December 18, Senator Arthur Vandenberg of Michigan told Stettinius, "The general sentiment in this country is that the president has completely turned the Polish situation over to Stalin to do anything he wants do with them."[51] When Stettinius met with the president on December 22, he more than likely repeated Vandenberg's criticism. The next day, the president left Washington by train to spend Christmas at Hyde Park. Before returning to the capital on Saturday, December 30, he received a cable from Stalin that left little doubt that the Soviet government was preparing to recognize a provisional Polish government of their creation which would be completely obedient to Moscow. On Saturday, December 30, Stettinius met with the president at the White House for approximately fifty minutes.

The vital matter of the president's response to Stalin's cable was not first on their agenda. They discussed what the president might say about foreign policy in his forthcoming State of the Union address. Stettinius informed the president of the results of a series of public opinion polls which indicated that the public's confidence in the president's handling of foreign policy was declining. In Stettinius' words, "The president and I [then] had a general discussion on other matters."[52] These other matters included a Jewish homeland in Palestine and Stettinius' wish to have briefing sessions with the president about the approaching summit meeting.

At the conclusion of this far-flung discussion, Stettinius asked Charles E. Bohlen to join them. Bohlen, who was then serving as a liaison between the State Department and the White House, had prepared a draft of a proposed response to Stalin's cable. He had included some strong language, stronger, perhaps, than any language that Roosevelt had ever used before in his cables to Stalin. Bohlen's draft read in part:

> I am disturbed and deeply disappointed over your message of December 27 in regard to Poland in which you tell me that you cannot see your way clear to hold in abeyance the question of recognizing the Lublin Committee as the provisional government of Poland until we have had an opportunity at our meeting to discuss the whole question thoroughly. . . . I had urged this delay upon you because I felt you would realize how extremely unfortunate and even serious it would be at this period in the war in its effect on world opinion and enemy morale if your government should formally recognize one government of Poland while the majority of the other United Nations including the United States and Great Britain continue to recognize and to maintain diplomatic relations with the Polish government in London. I

must tell you with a frankness equal to your own that I see no prospect of this government's following suit and transferring its recognition from the government in London to the Lublin Committee in its present form.[53]

In the remaining moments of their meeting, Roosevelt approved Bohlen's draft in its entirety, adding a final sentence that read, "I cannot, from a military angle, see any great objection to a delay of a month."[54]

It was far too little and much too late to change the course of events. Stalin gave short shrift to the president's plea. On January 5, 1945, the Soviet government recognized the Lublin Committee as the provisional government of Poland. It was the beginning of the end for the Polish government in London and for any real hope of a free and independent Poland. The loss of Poland as a free and independent state was a foreign policy failure of the first magnitude. Franklin Roosevelt and Cordell Hull both had a share in the responsibility for this failure.

Hull had been beguiled by Molotov and even more so by Stalin at the foreign ministers' meeting in Moscow. On his return to Washington, he confidently predicted that there would no longer be any need for "alliances." He told the members of Congress that Stalin was a "great statesman." Hull never fully understood the unpalatable truth that Stalin was a murderous tyrant. During 1944, Hull made almost no effort to develop a coherent foreign policy toward Poland or the rest of Eastern Europe. He never availed himself of the extraordinary experience and expertise of George F. Kennan, who understood Stalin better than anyone in the State Department. By October 1944, Hull physically could no longer carry on the duties of secretary of state. Finally, in November, he submitted his resignation. It would have been better for Hull, for his place in history, for Poland and for the United States if he had resigned the year before on his seventy-second birthday.

Unlike his secretary of state, Franklin Roosevelt understood, at the very least, that Stalin had been a murderous tyrant in the not-too-distant past. Roosevelt's self-confidence was such that he believed that through his own style of personal diplomacy he could bring Stalin into the fold of progressive world leaders. For years he had convinced himself that he could conduct foreign policy without the benefit of his secretary of state or career foreign service officers. In regard to Poland, Roosevelt never had any well-conceived policy. His tactical plan was to avoid any confrontation with Stalin and to put off most hard decisions until the Yalta Conference or the postwar peace conference. It was a tactic that gave all the advantages to Stalin.

Four years before Stalin's death, Eleanor Roosevelt published a book containing a few of her husband's private thoughts about the Soviet ruler.

> A remark made to him by Mr. Stalin in one of their talks stayed in his mind and I think gave him hope that there might be after the war more flexibility in communism or at least in that particular communist leader. . . . My husband said [to Stalin], "So much depends in the future on how we get along together. Do you think it will be possible for the United States and the USSR to see things in similar ways?" Mr. Stalin responded: "You have come a long way in the United States from your original concept of government and its responsibilities, and your original way of life. I think it is quite possible that we in the USSR, as our resources develop and people can have an easier life, will find ourselves growing nearer to some of your concepts and you may be finding yourselves accepting some of ours." . . . It did indicate a certain amount of flexibility and encouraged my husband to believe that confidence could be built between the leaders and that we might at least find a way to live in the world together, each country developing along the lines that seemed best for it.[55]

Mrs. Roosevelt also wrote of her husband's reaction to his first meeting with Stalin.

> My husband enjoyed his first contact with Stalin. It was always a challenge to him to meet new people whom he knew he had to win over to his own point of view, and this encounter was especially important. I know he was impressed by the strength of Marshal Stalin's personality. On his return he was always careful in describing him to mention that he was short and thick-set and powerful and gave the impression of being a bigger man than he actually was. He also said that his control over the people of his country was unquestionably due to their trust in him and their confidence that he had their good will at heart. It is hard to describe what gives a man the quality of leadership, but I am sure my husband felt that Marshal Stalin had this quality.[56]

Roosevelt's fatuous comments about Stalin and the Russian people's trust in him were largely overlooked by the American people at the time of the publication of his wife's book. In 1949, Americans still retained their image of Russia as a great, heroic ally. Fifty years later, the allure of Roosevelt's fame obscures his misadventures. It is, perhaps, ironic that one of the severest critics of Roosevelt's policy toward the Soviet Union is a Russian.

Aleksandr Solzhenitsyn was born in Rostov on December 11, 1918. After the German invasion in 1941, he volunteered for the army. From 1942 until 1945, he commanded an artillery battery at the front for which he was twice decorated. In 1945, in east Prussia, the twenty-six-year-old captain was arrested and sentenced to eight years of forced labor for derogatory remarks about "the man with the mustache" made in a letter to a friend. Solzhenitsyn was released from prison in 1953, following which he was exiled to Siberia for three years. His first book, *One Day in the Life of Ivan Denisovich*, was published in 1962. He published six more books before being expelled from the Soviet Union in 1974. In 1969, he was awarded the Paris Prix du Meilleur Livre Etranger. He received the Nobel Prize for Literature in 1970. Between 1973 and 1976 he published *The Gulag Archipelago* in three volumes. Since then he has produced another six books, including his autobiography. Solzhenitsyn's Russian citizenship was restored in 1990. That same year, he was awarded the Russian State Literature Prize. He is one of the great Russian writers of the twentieth century. He is a Russian patriot in the finest sense of the word.

In one of his novels, Solzhenitsyn has described the capricious nature of Stalin's hideous deeds in a way that few historians can equal.

> Stalin was terrifying because one mistake in his presence could be that one mistake in life which set off an explosion, irreversible in effect. Stalin was terrifying because he did not listen to excuses, made no accusations; his yellow tiger eyes simply brightened balefully, his lower lids closed up a bit—and there, inside him, sentence had been passed, and the condemned man didn't know: he left in peace, was arrested at night, and shot by morning.[57]

On December 27, 1979, Solzhenitsyn was residing in the United States in the state of Vermont. He soon learned that on that date the Soviet Union had launched its invasion of Afghanistan. Two months later, he completed a lengthy article titled "Misconceptions About Russia Are a Threat to America," which was published in the spring 1980 issue of *Foreign Affairs*. The Soviet invasion may well have convinced him to produce this critique.

In this article, Solzhenitsyn exposes Roosevelt's illusions about Stalin and communism in a way that few others ever have. He writes,

> And only by some evil figment of the imagination could Stalin be called a "Russian Nationalist"—this of the man who exterminated 15 million of the best Russian peasants, who broke the back of the Russian peasantry, and thereby of Russia herself, and who sacrificed the lives of more than 30 million people in the Second World War, which he waged without regard for less profligate means of warfare, without grudging the lives of the people.[58] . . . Many present and former U.S. diplomats have also used their office and authority to help enshroud Soviet communism in a dangerous, explosive cloud of vaporous arguments and illusions. Much of this legacy stems from such diplomats of the Roosevelt school as Averell Harriman, who to this day assures gullible Americans that the Kremlin rulers are peace-loving men . . .[59]
>
> And what of 1941–45? It was then that communism first succeeded in saddling and bridling Russian nationalism: millions of lives were affected and it took place in full view of the rest of the world, the murderer saddled his half-dead victim but in America or Britain no one was appalled; the whole western world responded with unanimous enthusiasm, and "Russia" was forgiven for all the unpleasant associations her name aroused and for all past sins and omissions. For the first time she became the object of infatuation and applause (paradoxically, even as she ceased being herself) because this saddle horse was then saving the western world from Hitler . . .[60] At the time the West refused even to entertain the thought that the Russians might have any feelings other than communist ones . . .[61]
>
> For the West, however, anyone who wanted to liberate himself from communism in that war was regarded as a traitor to the cause of the West. Every nation in the USSR could be wiped out for all the West cared, and any number of millions could die in Soviet concentration camps, just as long as it could get out of the war successfully and as quickly as possible. And so

hundreds of thousands of these Russians and Cossacks, Tartars and Caucasian nationals were sacrificed, they were not even allowed to surrender to the Americans, but were turned over to the Soviet Union, there to face reprisals and execution . . .[62]

At the same time it seemed more advantageous to buy off the communists with a couple of million foolish people and in this way to purchase perpetual peace. In the same way—and without any real need—the whole of eastern Europe was sacrificed to Stalin . . .[63]

The lesson of World War II is that only desperate, pitiless circumstances can bring about any cooperation between communism and the nation it has enslaved. The United States has not learned this lesson: The Soviet and eastern European governments have been treated as the genuine spokesmen of the national aspirations of the peoples they have subjugated, and the false representatives of these regimes have been dealt with respectfully . . .[64]

Communism will never be halted by negotiations or through the machinations of détente. It can be halted only by force from without or by disintegration from within.[65]

The American foreign policy failure in Poland was part of a larger foreign policy failure involving all of the oppressed peoples of Russia and Eastern Europe about whom Solzhenitsyn has written with such pain and such grief. In all this failure, the greatest tragedy involved Poland. The Second World War had started over Poland. On September 3, 1939, at 11:15 A.M. in a radio address, Prime Minister Neville Chamberlain had informed the British people that a state of war existed with Nazi Germany. The reason for this declaration of war was Germany's pre-dawn invasion of Poland on September 1, and its failure to comply with ultimatums from the governments of Britain and France to withdraw its forces from Polish territory forthwith.

No one can know with certainty how many men, women and children died during the Second World War. Scholars estimate that at least 50 million perished as a direct result of the war. Out of this total, more than 6 million were Polish men, women and children. In Warsaw alone, 700,000 people lost their lives, more than the combined losses of the United Kingdom and the United States of America. Out of Poland's prewar population of 35 million, 17 percent had lost their lives. In comparison, the total war-related deaths in the USSR were 20 million, representing slightly less than 12 percent of its prewar population.

The percentages of the Polish intelligentsia who lost their lives were much higher. Poland lost 45 percent of its physicians and dentists, 57 percent of its lawyers and 40 percent of its university professors. By the end of the twentieth century, Poland again had become a sovereign, independent nation, but it had taken almost fifty years for it to become free. For that catastrophe, Cordell Hull and Franklin Roosevelt cannot be held blameless.

Vice Admiral Ross T. McIntire, the protagonist in the colossal deceit that President Roosevelt's health remained excellent.

Presidential advisor Samuel Rosenman and FDR's cardiologist Dr. Howard G. Bruenn. In 1970 Dr. Bruenn revealed to the medical world the disturbing details of FDR's heart condition.

CHAPTER EIGHT

Epilogue

In February 1945, Anna Boettiger was invited by her father to accompany him to Yalta. This had been humiliating to Eleanor Roosevelt, who had wanted to go. Her husband had brushed aside her request to accompany him with the explanation that it would be better for Anna to go because everyone would make a lot less fuss over her. This was hardly the complete explanation. More than ever the president needed the presence of someone who could give him emotional support. For this reason, he chose his daughter over his wife.

After reaching the Crimea, Lieutenant Commander Bruenn decided to ignore Admiral McIntire's admonition to remain silent. He told Anna of the serious nature of her father's heart condition. She immediately wrote her husband that her father's condition was far more serious than she had ever known.

Just before the Yalta Conference, Churchill's physician had learned of Roosevelt's heart problem from a prominent American doctor. Dr. Roger Lee of Boston, a former president of the American College of Physicians and the American Medical Association, had written Lord Moran:

> Roosevelt had heart failure eight months ago. There are, of course, degrees of congestive failure, but Roosevelt had enlargement of his liver and was puffy. A post-mortem would have shown congestion of his organs. He was irascible and became very irritable if he had to concentrate his mind for long. If anything was brought up that wanted thinking out he would change the subject. He was, too, sleeping badly.[1]

Some photographs of the president taken at Yalta revealed the face of a shockingly ill man. A few days after the Conference ended, Churchill met Roosevelt on the cruiser *Quincy* in Alexandria Harbor. Afterward, Churchill wrote:

> . . . shortly before noon I went on board for what was to be my last talk with the President. We gathered afterwards in his cabin for an informal family luncheon. I was accompanied by Sarah and Randolph, and Mr. Roosevelt's daughter, Mrs. Boettiger, joined us, together with Harry Hopkins and Mr. Winant. The President seemed placid and frail. I felt that he had a slender contact with life.[2]

On April 12, 1945, at Warm Springs, President Roosevelt suddenly died of a cerebral hemorrhage. The tragedy could have been far worse for the nation. If Roosevelt had survived the stroke, its effects could have left him *non compos mentis*. Secretary of the Treasury Henry Morgenthau Jr. had been with Roosevelt the night before he died. Five days later he recorded his private doubts about statements that McIntire was giving out:

> This commander in the Navy who attended him is a heart man from the Presbyterian Hospital, but I gathered that Admiral McIntire was telling everybody in the train that this was wholly unexpected, and that they hadn't looked for it, which, of course, is just sheer damn nonsense because I have

heard from two or three sources that the President had an enlarged heart.[3]

In 1946, McIntire, who had been the president's official physician for more than twelve years, wrote his only book, *White House Physician.* The title page informs the reader that it was written in collaboration with George Creel. Under their arrangement, McIntire instructed Creel on the theme and tone of his book. He also furnished Creel with the raw material, including the clinical details of Roosevelt's medical history. The actual drafting was done by Creel, a journalist who had published more than half a dozen books.

Their collaboration turned sour. Creel was satisfied with neither the quality nor the quantity of the raw material from McIntire. He also discovered that McIntire was indifferent to the publisher's deadline, which was June 1, 1946.

If the admiral had ever intended to write an accurate account of President Roosevelt's condition, he would have contacted Dr. Bruenn. It is doubtful that they saw one another after Bruenn was released from active duty with the Navy in February 1946. While Howard Creel was struggling in New York City to draft a satisfactory manuscript, the one person who knew more about Roosevelt's medical condition than anyone else was also in New York City. In May, Howard Bruenn resumed his cardiology practice at 903 Park Avenue. At the same time, he returned to the staff of Columbia Presbyterian. In June, he moved his wife, who was expecting their third child that month, and their two young children from Rockville, Maryland, to Riverdale, New York.

In August, Bruenn received a two-page letter from McIntire, who promised him a copy of his book as soon as it was off the press. McIntire also indicated that he wanted Bruenn's opinion on the book's merit. Bruenn could never bring himself to tell the admiral what he really thought.

A few months later, *White House Physician* was released by Putnam's. It is a book of 244 pages, without photographs. It has no foreword, no bibliography and no index. While *White House Physician* seemed to confirm that Roosevelt from time to time discussed matters of state with McIntire, which might justify its publication, the book's ultimate worth depended on whether it gave posterity a totally candid picture of Franklin Roosevelt's state of health. By this standard, the book was an abject failure.

The flagrant misrepresentations found in *White House Physician* seemed credible enough at the time because they were entirely consistent with McIntire's previous false statements. The book's most egregious misrepresentations are the following:

> . . . that stout heart of his never failed.[4]
> The President . . . never had any serious heart condition . . .[5]

> They [his statements to the press] were not glowing in the sense that they painted the President as a perfect physical specimen but a cautious judgment that he was in "excellent condition for a man of his age." *I stand by that judgment today without amendment or apology.*[6]

> His blood pressure was not alarming at any time . . .[7]

> To my consternation it had been arranged for him to speak from the forecastle deck of a destroyer . . . A stiff wind was blowing, and there was quite a slant to the deck, two things that called for bracing on his part, and as a result he finished up with considerable pain. Purely muscular as it turned out . . .[8]

This last excerpt relates to the president's speech from the bridge of the destroyer *Cummings* on August 12, 1944, when the president experienced severe pain in his chest and shoulder. After examining the president, Bruenn diagnosed the condition as angina pectoris resulting from insufficient blood reaching the heart. It is inconceivable that McIntire was misinformed about Bruenn's diagnosis.

There are questionable features to McIntire's book outside the medical realm. If Churchill ever read *White House Physician*, which is highly unlikely, he would have been astounded by McIntire's use of a phrase that Churchill had made historic with his speech at Fulton, Missouri, on March 5, 1946, at least six months before McIntire's book was published. The phrase in question was "iron curtain." McIntire implied that he had coined this phrase at Yalta in February 1945. His book states:

I had become fairly friendly with some of the Russian officers and one conversation in particular was most enlightening.
"Why," I asked them, "do you still keep your Iron Curtain? What
is your idea in refusing to let the Americans and the British get
behind it? Don't you trust us?"[9]

McIntire's book was reviewed in the winter 1947 issue of *The Virginia Quarterly
Review* by Ernest K. Lindley, who was then chief of the Washington Bureau of
Newsweek. Lindley made no attempt to second-guess McIntire on Roosevelt's state
of health, but he did make a perceptive comment on McIntire's motive for writing
this book. Lindley observed, " 'White House Physician' is by implication a defense
of his public statements on Roosevelt's physical condition, especially during the
1944 campaign."[10]

Several years after McIntire's death in 1959, Anna and her husband, Dr. James
Halsted, a professor of clinical medicine at Albany Medical College, became
aggrieved about unending speculation regarding her father's illnesses. Anna had
befriended Howard Bruenn, who was her age, during the year that Bruenn had
treated her father. After Bruenn resumed his medical practice in New York, they
kept in touch. The Halsteds decided that the best way to set the record straight
would be to have Bruenn publish a totally candid account of her father's final illness.
It was only after she had obtained the consent of her four brothers that Bruenn felt
comfortable with this task.

He started by reviewing his handwritten clinical notes. Bruenn had followed the
practice every day that he saw Roosevelt of making two sets of clinical notes, one for
the president's hospital chart and one for his own records. Bruenn, then at the height
of his career as a highly respected cardiologist, was extremely busy. It took him over two
years to complete his manuscript. He was well aware that this article would be scruti-
nized by the Roosevelt family, by the medical profession and by historians. He was
determined to publish his work in a respected medical journal. By early 1970, Bruenn
felt satisfied with his effort. His article appeared in the April 1970 issue of *Annals of
Internal Medicine* under the title "Clinical Notes on the Illness and Death of President
Franklin D. Roosevelt."

The lead paragraph of Bruenn's article contained a stunning disclosure. It
revealed that the president's official medical records had disappeared shortly after his

death. Bruenn's carefully chosen words read: "The original hospital chart in which all clinical notes as well as the results of the various laboratory tests were incorporated was kept in the safe at the U.S. Naval Hospital, Bethesda, Md. After the president's death this chart could not be found."[11] Bruenn offered no opinion on whether the president's medical records had been deliberately destroyed.

Bruenn's article includes the clinical details of the president's condition on March 27, 1944, which was the first time that he had seen Roosevelt professionally. He wrote:

> Physical examination on March 27, 1944 showed a temperature of 99F by mouth, pulse of 72/min. and respiration of 24/min. He appeared to be very tired and his face was very gray. Moving caused considerable breathlessness . . . Percussion showed the apex of the heart to be in the sixth interspace, 2 cm to the left of the midclavicular line, suggesting an enlarged heart . . . Blood pressure was 186/108mm Hg. . . . An electrocardiogram showed sinus rhythm with deep inversion of the T waves in leads 1 and CF₄ . . .Fluoroscopy and X-rays of the chest showed a considerable increase in the size of the cardiac shadow, as measured in the anterior-posterior position . . . The great vessel shadow was also increased in size. This enlargement was apparently due to a diffusely dilated and tortuous aorta, including the ascending, arch and thoracic portions. The pulmonary vessels were engorged.[12]

1944
186/108

Bruenn publicly revealed the diagnosis he had made privately twenty-six years before. "Accordingly, a diagnosis was made of hypertension, hypertensive heart disease, cardiac failure (left ventricular), and acute bronchitis. These findings and their interpretation was [sic] conveyed to Surgeon General McIntire. They had been completely unsuspected up to this time."[13]

Bruenn further revealed that throughout 1944, the president's blood pressure was alarmingly high. On April 1, he examined the president at the White House. His blood pressure was 192 to 200/106 to 108mm Hg. On April 4, following a good night's sleep, his blood pressure was 222 to 226/118 mm Hg. Three weeks later at Hobcaw plantation in South Carolina, the president experienced what may have been a gall bladder attack. That day his blood pressure was 230/120 mm Hg. Four days later, when he again had abdominal pain, his blood pressure was at 240/130 mm Hg.

In September, at the Quebec Conference, Bruenn noted that the president's blood pressure was higher than usual after he had viewed the film *Wilson*. Roosevelt, who had served in President Wilson's administration, knew all too well the effects of Wilson's stroke. During that conference, the president's blood pressure ranged from 180/100 to 240/130 mm Hg. One of the highest blood pressure readings ever noted by Bruenn occurred in November at Warm Springs, after the president had engaged in mild swimming in an indoor, heated pool. It was 260/150 mm Hg. Bruenn called it "an alarming rise."[14]

In 1990, five years before Bruenn's death, Jan Kenneth Herman, the editor of *Navy Medicine,* a bimonthly publication of the U.S. Navy's Bureau of Medicine and Surgery, interviewed him. Herman has said that at the time of this interview, Bruenn's memory was excellent. The following questions and answers speak for themselves:

> Herman: McIntire was the spokesman on the President's health and everyone was saying that the President didn't look well, what was wrong with him, and he would say, "It's nothing, it's simply an upper respiratory thing, he's had the flu or a case of bronchitis," or whatever. He really couldn't say anything else. All this I can understand—politics. What I have difficulty with is reading McIntire's book, which he wrote in 1946. In it he maintained, to the bitter end, that the President was essentially a healthy man for his age. His blood pressure was normal. His heart signs were normal and everything else was normal. While the President was alive, for political reasons, McIntire had to maintain a positive image. But once FDR was dead and a whole year had gone by, McIntire felt compelled to write his memoir and in it he goes through the whole litany all over again. Can you think of why he did that?
>
> Bruenn: I didn't publish my paper until 1970 and that sort of blew the door down as far as the actual facts were concerned.
>
> Herman: So, it wasn't really until 1970 that any of this came out?
>
> Bruenn: That's right. There was always the question of violating the relationship between the patient and a doctor. Anna [Roosevelt] really went after me to write this thing but got per-

mission from her three [*sic*] brothers—they all thought it was
a pretty good idea—just to clarify the situation. There were so
many rumors, even years after his death. For example, the
Russians wanted to have an autopsy; they thought he had
been poisoned or something of the sort. So I did write it on
the basis that the family wanted me to. The editors of the
journal agreed. I must have gotten over 150 requests for
reprints of that article.

My contact with McIntire stopped when I left the Navy.
We communicated letters, but nothing about this.

Herman: The thing that has bothered historians, and you
mention it in your paper, is the fact that FDR's medical
records have disappeared.

Bruenn: It's one of the strangest things. When I'd come
back [from seeing the president at the White House] I would
go to Dr. Harper's (4) office or Duncan's (5) office and they
would give me the chart, and I would write a note for the day
concerning what I'd found, return it to the administrative
office, and then it would go back in the safe. After I wrote the
final note, I never saw it again, never saw it. You might find it
in your files, I'm not sure.

Herman: It's gone.

Bruenn: Isn't that curious.

Herman: I suspect, well it's all circumstantial, but the person who had the most to lose from those records being made
public was Dr. McIntire.

Bruenn: That's right.

Herman: He really took a risk during the President's life
choosing to keep the whole thing bottled up. In 1946, he really went out on a limb, thinking, of course, that this material
would never be divulged, by saying the president was perfectly
healthy. The fact that he looked tired was not abnormal for a
man with his responsibility. "Besides, he didn't follow my
advice. I told him to rest and he couldn't. He was the
President." But there was nothing organically wrong with him.
McIntire said it time and time again. I can't imagine him ever
wanting those records to see the light of day.

Bruenn: Sure, I don't see how anyone other than somebody
in some official position could have gotten their hands on them.
Well, it's one of those mysteries.[15]

There is no doubt that McIntire had easy access to the president's medical records. Although the commanding officer of the Bethesda Naval Hospital and his executive officer also had access to the safe where these records were kept, they had no motive to destroy them. McIntire clearly did have a motive to destroy them. His feelings about Roosevelt had bordered on adulation. He convinced himself that his president was indispensable to his country and to the world. In 1944, he had lied to the American people about the president's health in order to scotch the only issue that could have cost FDR the election. *White House Physician* repeated these lies in order to dispel doubts about McIntire's credibility. At Mrs. Roosevelt's request, there had been no autopsy. McIntire clearly wanted his book to be the final word on the president's health. Since the president's official medical records had vanished the year before the publication of *White House Physician,* it might well have been the final word. McIntire had convinced himself that no one could expose his fraud without the official records. He had failed to consider the possibility that Bruenn had kept a duplicate set of clinical notes.

Few historians have conducted a more diligent search for FDR's missing medical records than Jan Kenneth Herman, who was recently the historian for the Navy's Bureau of Medicine and Surgery in Washington, D.C. His quest has taken him to the National Military Personnel Records Center in St. Louis, Missouri, and to the Franklin D. Roosevelt Library in Hyde Park, New York. Herman has not been able to find any trace of them. He believes that these records were deliberately destroyed. He has little doubt about the identity of the person responsible.

In 1944, Vice Admiral Ross T. McIntire successfully deceived the American people about their president's health. After Roosevelt's death, McIntire, through his book, tried to deceive history. This calculated, self-serving scheme did not succeed because of two people who insisted on the truth about Roosevelt's precarious state of health. They were Anna Roosevelt Halsted and Howard G. Bruenn, to whom all those with a serious interest in the life of Franklin Delano Roosevelt should be forever grateful.

The lessons from Roosevelt's decline in 1944 are clear. First and foremost, a president must face the truth about his health. Second, barring highly unusual circumstances, a president must make a complete and full disclosure of his medical condition to the American people. President Roosevelt had followed a different course. He had condoned one of Admiral McIntire's most misleading public statements about his health. He had never asked his cardiologist, Dr. Bruenn, anything about his heart condition. During much of 1944, he had been indifferent to the horrific risk that a heart attack or stroke could leave him mentally incompetent. This lapse of judgment, perhaps more than anything else, reveals the extent of his decline.

SOURCE NOTES

CHAPTER ONE

1 James Roosevelt and Sidney Shalett, *Affectionately, FDR, a Son's Story of a Lonely Man* (New York: Harcourt, Brace & Company, 1959), p. 319.

2 Frances Perkins, *The Roosevelt I Knew* (New York: Viking Press, 1946), p. 3.

3 Robert E. Sherwood, *Roosevelt and Hopkins, an Intimate History* (New York: Harper & Brothers, 1948), p. 9.

4 Lois Gordon and Alan Gordon, *Six Decades in American Life 1920–1980, American Chronicle* (New York: Atheneum, 1987), p. 119.

5 Irwin Glusker and Richard M. Ketchum (editors), *American Testament: Fifty Great Documents of American History* (New York: American Heritage Publishing Co., 1971), p. 192.

6 Ross T. McIntire, *White House Physician* (New York: G. P. Putnam's Sons, 1946), p. 101.

7 Ibid., p. 139

8 Ibid., pp. 175–76.

CHAPTER TWO

1   Margaret Suckley, *Closest Companion,* edited and annotated by Geoffrey C. Ward (New York: Houghton Mifflin Company, 1995), p. 267.

2   Ibid.

3   Ross T. McIntire, *White House Physician* (New York: G. P. Putnam's Sons, 1946), p. 75.

4   Ibid., p. 137.

5   Ibid., p. 56.

6   Ibid., p. 64.

7   Ibid., p. 15.

8   Robert E. Sherwood, *Roosevelt and Hopkins: an Intimate History* (New York: Harper & Brothers, 1948), p. 671, pp. 672–73.

9   Russell D. Buhite and David W. Levy, editors, *FDR's Fireside Chats* (Norman: University of Oklahoma Press, 1992), p. 283.

10   McIntire, *White House Physician,* p. 182.

11   Suckley, *Closest Companion,* p. 271.

12   Ibid., p. 280.

13   Ibid., p. 288.

14   Grace Tully, *FDR My Boss* (New York: Charles Scribner's Sons, 1949), p. 274.

15   Howard G. Bruenn, *Navy Medicine Magazine,* vol. 81, no. 2, March–April 1990, p. 8.

16   Ibid.

17   Ibid., pp. 8–9

18   Bernard M. Baruch, *The Public Years* (New York: Holt, Rinehart and Winston, 1960), pp. 335–36.

19   Turner Catledge, *My Life and the Times* (New York: Harper & Row, 1971), p. 144

20   Ibid., p. 146.

21   Suckley, *Closest Companion,* p. 293.

22   Ibid., p. 295.

23   Ibid., p. 296.

24   George McJimsey, *Harry Hopkins: Ally of the Poor and Defender of Democracy* (Cambridge, Mass.: Harvard University Press, 1987), p. 317.

25 William D. Hassett, *Off the Record with FDR 1942–1945* (New Brunswick, NJ: Rutgers University Press, 1958), p. 243.

26 Stephen Early Collection, Press and Radio Conference, 3:45 P.M., Box 42, 6/8/44 (FDR Library, Hyde Park, N.Y.).

27 McIntire, *White House Physician*, p. 194.

28 James Roosevelt and Sidney Shalett, *Affectionately, FDR, a Son's Story of a Lonely Man* (New York: Harcourt, Brace & Company, 1959), p. 352.

29 Ernest J. King and Walter Muir Whitehill, *Fleet Admiral King: A Naval Record* (New York: W. W. Norton & Company, 1952), p. 568.

30 Ibid.

31 Douglas MacArthur, *Reminiscences* (New York: McGraw-Hill Book Company, 1964), pp. 198–99.

32 Ibid., p. 199.

33 Bruenn, *Navy Medicine Magazine*, vol. 81, no. 2, March–April 1990, p. 9.

34 Suckley, *Closest Companion*, p. 321.

35 George Tames, *Eye on Washington, the Presidents Who Have Known Me* (New York: Harper Collins, 1990), p. 20.

36 McIntire, *White House Physician*, p. 204.

37 Lord Moran, *Churchill Taken from the Diaries of Lord Moran* (Boston: Houghton Mifflin Company, 1966), p. 192.

38 Catledge, *My Life and the Times*, p. 149.

39 Joseph P. Kennedy, *Hostage to Fortune, The Letters of Joseph P. Kennedy,* edited by Amanda Smith (New York: Viking Penguin, 2001), p. 607.

40 Ibid., p. 612.

41 Suckley, *Closest Companion*, p. 348.

42 Ibid., pp. 362–63.

43 Hassett, *Off the Record with F. D. R.,* p. 282.

44 Ibid., p. 307.

CHAPTER THREE

1 Henry A. Wallace, *The Price of Vision, The Diary of Henry A. Wallace 1942–1946,* (Boston: Houghton Mifflin Company, 1973), pp. 308–9.

2   Roger Biles, *The Mayors—The Chicago Political Tradition, Revised Edition*, edited by Paul M. Green and Melvin G. Holli (Carbondale and Edwardsville: Southern Illinois University Press, 1995), p. 111.

3   Harold L. Ickes, *The Secret Diary of Harold L. Ickes, Volume III, The Lowering Clouds 1939–1941* (New York: Simon & Schuster, 1954), p. 94.

4   Sidney Fine, *The Supreme Court Justices Illustrated Biographies 1789–1993*, edited by Clare Cushman (Washington: Congressional Quarterly, 1993), p. 398.

5   Ickes, *Secret Diary*, pp. 278–79.

6   Wallace, *The Price of Vision*, pp. 189–90.

7   James F. Byrnes, *All in One Lifetime* (New York: Harper & Brothers, 1958), p. 217.

8   Edward J. Flynn, *You're the Boss, My Story of a Life in Practical Politics* (New York: Viking Press, 1947), p. 174.

9   Byrnes, *All In One Lifetime*, p. 218.

10 Flynn, *You're the Boss*, pp. 177–78.

11 Wallace, *The Price of Vision*, p. 295.

12 William D. Leahy, *I Was There* (New York: Whittlesey House, McGraw-Hill Book Company, 1950), p. 239.

13 Margaret Suckley, edited and annotated by Geoffrey C. Ward, *Closest Companion* (New York: Houghton Mifflin Company, 1995), pp. 301–2.

14 Flynn, *You're the Boss*, p. 181.

15 Byrnes, *All in One Lifetime*, p. 177.

16 David McCullough, *Truman* (New York: Simon & Schuster, 1992), p. 301.

17 Ibid.

18 Wallace, *The Price of Vision*, pp. 365–66, n.1.

19 Ibid., p. 364.

20 Harry S. Truman, *Dear Bess—The Letters from Harry to Bess Truman, 1910–1959*, edited by Robert H. Ferrell (New York: W. W. Norton and Company, 1983), p. 505.

21 Byrnes, *All in One Lifetime*, p. 224.

22 Ibid.

23 Suckley, *Closest Companion*, supra, pp. 318–19.

24 Byrnes, *All in One Lifetime*, supra. p. 226.

25 Ibid.

26 Ibid., p. 227.

27 Leahy, *I Was There,* pp. 247–48.

28 Samuel I. Rosenman, *Working with Roosevelt* (New York: Harper & Brothers, 1952), pp. 449-50.

29 Grace Tully, *FDR My Boss* (New York: Charles Scribner's Sons, 1949), p. viii.

30 Ibid., p. 276.

31 James Roosevelt and Sidney Shalett, *Affectionately FDR, a Son's Story of a Lonely Man* (New York: Harcourt, Brace & Company, 1959), p. 351.

32 Bernard M. Baruch, *Baruch: The Public Years* (New York: Holt, Rinehart and Winston, 1960), p. 339.

CHAPTER FOUR

1 Charles E. Bohlen, *Witness to History 1929–1969* (New York: W. W. Norton, 1973), p. 122.

2 David Cannadine, editor, *Blood, Toil, Tears and Sweat, The Speeches of Winston Churchill* (Boston: Houghton Mifflin Company, 1989), pp. 157, 160, 165.

3 Robert E. Sherwood, *Roosevelt and Hopkins, an Intimate History* (New York: Harper Brothers, 1948), pp. 181–82.

4 Ibid., p. 222.

5 Warren F. Kimball, editor, *Churchill and Roosevelt, The Complete Correspondence,* volume I (Norwalk, Connecticut: Easton Press, 1995), pp. 108–09.

6 Russell D. Buhite and David W. Levy, editors, *FDR's Fireside Chats* (New York: Penguin Books, 1993), pp. 170, 171, 173.

7 Winston S. Churchill, *The Second World War*** The Grand Alliance* (Boston: Houghton Mifflin Company, 1950), p. 23.

8 Bohlen, *Witness to History,* p. 148.

9 Winston S. Churchill, *The Second World War****** Triumph and Tragedy,* (Boston: Houghton Mifflin Company, 1953) p. 149.

10 Ibid., p. 161.

11 Sherwood, *Roosevelt and Hopkins,* p. xvi.

12 Joseph P. Lash, *Eleanor Roosevelt: A Friend's Memoir* (Garden City, NY: Doubleday & Company, 1964), p. 212.

13   Eleanor Roosevelt, *This I Remember* (New York: Harper Brothers, 1949), p. 335.

14   Ibid., p. 275.

15   Ibid.

16   Ibid.

17   Henry A. Wallace, *The Price of Vision, The Diary of Henry A. Wallace, 1942–1946* (Boston: Houghton Mifflin Company, 1973), p. 145.

18   William D. Leahy, *I Was There* (New York: Whittlesey House, 1950), p. 265.

19   Henry A. Adams, *Harry Hopkins: A Biography* (New York: G. P. Putnam's Sons, 1977), p. 368.

20   Wallace, *The Price of Vision,* p. 140.

21   Ibid., pp. 289–90.

22   Ibid., pp. 369–70.

23   Edward J. Flynn, *You're the Boss* (New York: Viking Press, 1947), p. 156.

24   Letter from Brendan V. Sullivan Jr. for Williams & Connolly to Matthew B. Wills dated 4/23/96.

25   Sherwood, *Roosevelt and Hopkins,* p. 833.

26   Ibid., p. 819.

27   Dean Acheson, *Present at the Creation* (New York: W. W. Norton & Company, 1969), p. 9.

28   Sir Alexander Cadogan, *The Diaries of Sir Alexander Cadogan 1938–1945,* edited by David Dilks (New York: G. P. Putnam's Sons, 1972), p. 553.

CHAPTER FIVE

1   Winston S. Churchill, *The Second World War*** The Grand Alliance* (Boston: Houghton Mifflin Company, 1950), p. 23.

2   Elliott Roosevelt, *As He Saw It* (New York: Duell, Sloan and Pearce, 1946), pp. 204–5.

3   Dean Acheson, *Present at the Creation* (New York: W. W. Norton & Company, 1969), pp. 133–34.

4   Warren F. Kimball, editor, *Churchill and Roosevelt, The Complete Correspondence, III Alliance Declining* (Norwalk, Connecticut: Easton Press, 1995), pp. 6–7.

5   Ibid., p. 3.

6   Ibid., p. 140.

7   Warren F. Kimball, editor, *Churchill and Roosevelt, The Complete Correspondence, II Alliance Forged,* (Norwalk, Connecticut: Easton Press, 1995), p. 734.

8   Ibid., pp. 744–45.

9   Charles E. Bohlen, *Witness to History 1929–1969* (New York: W. W. Norton & Company, 1973), p. 151.

10 W. Averell Harriman and Elie Abel, *Special Envoy to Churchill and Stalin 1941–1946* (New York: Random House, 1975), p. 279.

11 Kimball, editor, *The Complete Correspondence III,* p. 61.

12 Churchill, *The Grand Alliance,* p. 443.

13 Kimball, editor, *The Complete Correspondence III,* pp. 70–71.

14 Ibid., p. 120.

15 Ibid., p. 139.

16 Ibid., p. 212.

17 Ibid., p. 219.

18 Nigel Nicolson, *Alex: The Life of Field Marshal Earl Alexander of Tunis* (New York: Atheneum, 1993), p. 259.

19 Arthur Bryant, *Triumph in the West, A History of the War Years Based on the Diaries of Field Marshal Lord Alanbrooke, Chief of the Imperial General Staff,* (Garden City, NY: Doubleday & Company, 1959), p. 167.

20 Kimball, editor, *The Complete Correspondence, III,* p. 227

21 John Keegan, *The Second World War* (New York: Penguin Books, 1990), p. 362.

22 Bryant, *Triumph in the West,* p. 188.

23 John Colville, *The Fringes of Power, 10 Downing Street Diaries 1939–1955,* (London: W. W. Norton & Company, 1985), p. 505.

24 Kimball, editor, *The Complete Correspondence III,* p. 295.

25 Ibid., p. 296.

26 Winston S. Churchill, *The Second World War****** Triumph and Tragedy* (Boston: Houghton Mifflin Company, 1953), pp. 140–41.

27 Ibid., p. 155.

28 Kimball, editor, *The Complete Correspondence III,* p. 322.

29 Colville, *The Fringes of Power,* p. 515.

30 Kimball, editor, *The Complete Correspondence, III*, p. 318.

31 Ibid., p. 383.

32 David Dimbleby and David Reynold, *An Ocean Apart—The Relationship Between Britain and America in the Twentieth Century* (New York: Random House, 1988), p. 176.

33 Edward R. Stettinius Jr., edited by Thomas M. Campbell and George C. Herring, *The Diaries of Edward R. Stettinius Jr., 1943–1946,* (New York: New Viewpoints, 1975), pp. 175–76.

34 Kimball, editor, *The Complete Correspondence, III*, p. 407.

35 Ibid.

36 Colville, *The Fringes of Power*, p. 528.

37 Ibid.

38 Thomas B. Buell, *Master of Sea Power, A Biography of Fleet Admiral Ernest J. King* (Boston: Little, Brown and Company, 1980), p. 179.

39 Ibid.

40 Viscount Cunningham, *A Sailor's Odyssey* (New York: E. P. Dutton & Company, 1951), pp. 450–66.

41 Forrest C. Pogue, editor, *George C. Marshall Interviews and Reminiscences for Forrest C. Pogue* (Lexington, Virginia: George C. Marshall Research Foundation, 1991), p. 593.

42 Robert E. Sherwood, *Roosevelt and Hopkins, an Intimate History* (New York: Harper & Brothers, 1948), pp. 840–41.

43 Ibid.

44 Cable from Earl of Halifax to Foreign Office, 10 December 1944, Public Record Office, Kew, Richmond, Surrey TW94DU Reference Prem 3/212/5 29675.

45 Cable from Prime Minister to Harry Hopkins 11 December 1994, Public Record Office, Kew, Richmond, Surrey TW94DU Reference T 2321/4.

46 Kimball, editor, *The Complete Correspondence, III*, p. 454.

47 Roosevelt, *As He Saw It*, pp. 222–23.

48 Summary of telegrams for the president, November 17, 1944, 7:00 A.M., President's Secretary's Files Collection, Box No. 73, Hyde Park, New York: Franklin D. Roosevelt Library.

49   James Forrestal Papers, Princeton University, Princeton, New Jersey: Seeley G. Mudd Manuscript Library.

CHAPTER SIX

1   Barbara W. Tuchman, *Stilwell and the America Experience in China 1911– 45* (New York: Macmillan, 1970), p. 15.

2   Ibid., p. 125.

3   Winston S. Churchill, *The Second World War**** The Hinge of Fate* (Boston: Houghton Mifflin Company, 1950), p. 144.

4   Joseph W. Stilwell, arranged and edited by Theodore H. White, *The Stilwell Papers* (New York: William Sloane Associates, 1948), p. 36.

5   Ibid., p. 37.

6   Ibid., p. 36.

7   Tuchman, *Stilwell and the American Experience in China*, p. 267.

8   Field Marshal the Viscount Slim, *Defeat into Victory* (New York: David McKay Company, 1961), p. 20.

9   Ibid., pp. 35–36.

10   Ibid., p. 58.

11   Ibid., p. 86.

12   Ibid.

13   Tuchman, *Stilwell and the America Experience in China*, p. 300.

14   Slim, *Defeat into Victory*, p. 118.

15   Robert E. Sherwood, *Roosevelt and Hopkins, an Intimate History* (New York: Harper & Brothers, 1948), p. 661.

16   Eleanor Roosevelt, *This I Remember* (New York: Harper & Brothers, 1949), p. 283.

17   Ibid., pp. 283–84.

18   Sherwood, *Roosevelt and Hopkins*, p. 706.

19   Stilwell, *The Stilwell Papers*, pp. 204–06.

20   Ibid., p. 246.

21   Elliott Roosevelt, *As He Saw It* (New York: Duell Sloan and Pearce, 1946), pp. 160–62.

22 John MacDonald, *Great Battles of World War II* (New York: Macmillan, 1986), p. 131.

23 Stilwell, *The Stilwell Papers,* p. 285.

24 Ibid.

25 Ibid., p. 286.

26 Slim, *Defeat into Victory,* pp. 261–62.

27 Cable from FDR to Chiang dated July 6, 1944, Map Room Collection, Box No. 10, FDR Library, Hyde Park, New York.

28 Written order from FDR to Hurley, dated August 12, 1944, President's Secretary's File, Box No. 138, FDR Library, Hyde Park, New York.

29 Stilwell, *Stilwell Papers,* p. 327.

30 Ibid., p. 330.

31 Cable from FDR to Chiang, dated September 16, 1944, Map Room Collection, Box No. 10, FDR Library, Hyde Park, New York.

32 Stilwell, *The Stilwell Papers,* p. 333.

33 Draft of proposed message from FDR to Chiang by Marshall, Marshall Papers, Box 81, Folder 23, George C. Marshall Research Foundation, Lexington, Virginia.

34 Stilwell, *Stilwell Papers,* p. 339

35 Ibid., pp. 340–41.

36 Cable from Hurley to FDR, dated October 13, 1944, Map Room Collection, Box No. 11, FDR Library, Hyde Park, New York.

37 W. Averell Harriman and Ellie Abel, *Special Envoy to Churchill and Stalin 1941–1946* (New York: Random House, 1975), pp. 370–71.

38 Henry A. Wallace, *The Price of Vision: The Diary of Henry A. Wallace 1942–1946,* (Boston: Houghton Mifflin Company, 1973), p. 411.

39 Henry C. Stimson and McGeorge Bundy, *On Active Service in Peace and War* (New York: Harper & Brothers, 1947), p. 539.

40 Theodore H. White, *In Search of History: A Personal Adventure* (New York: Harper & Row, 1978), p. 159.

41 Ibid., p. 166.

42 Ibid., p. 178–79.

CHAPTER SEVEN

1 Warren F. Kimball, editor, *Churchill and Roosevelt, The Complete Correspondence II, Alliance Forged* (Norwalk, Conn.: Easton Press, 1995), p. 389.

2 Winston S. Churchill, *The Second World War***** Closing the Ring* (Boston: Houghton Mifflin Company, 1951), p. 691.

3 Kimball, editor, *The Complete Correspondence II*, pp. 390–99.

4 W. Averell Harriman and Elie Abel, *Special Envoy to Churchill and Stalin 1941–1946* (New York: Random House, 1975), p. 302.

5 Frank Freidel, *Franklin D. Roosevelt, A Rendezvous with Destiny* (Boston: Little, Brown and Company, 1990), p. 329.

6 Dean Acheson, *Present at the Creation* (New York: W. W. Norton and Company, 1961), p. 12.

7 Cordell Hull, *The Memoirs of Cordell Hull, Volume II* (New York: Macmillan, 1948), p. 1278.

8 Ibid., p. 1292.

9 Ibid., p. 1294.

10 Ibid., p. 1308.

11 Ibid.

12 Ibid.

13 Ibid., p. 1309.

14 Ibid., p. 1311.

15 Ibid., p. 1313.

16 Ibid., p. 1305.

17 Ibid., p. 1448.

18 Ibid., p. 1313.

19 Anthony Eden, *The Memoirs of Anthony Eden, Earl of Avon, The Reckoning* (Boston: Houghton Mifflin Company, 1965), p. 482.

20 Hull, *Memoirs, Volume II*, pp. 1314–15.

21 Ibid., p. 1467.

22 Robert Murphy, *Diplomat among Warriors* (Garden City, New York: Doubleday and Company, 1964), p. 208.

23 Stanislaw Mikolajczyk, *The Rape of Poland* (New York: McGraw-Hill Book Company, 1948), p. 59.

24 Ibid.

25 Ibid.

26 Ibid., p. 82.

27 Hull, *Memoirs, Volume II*, p. 1446.

28 Warren F. Kimball, editor, *Churchill and Roosevelt, The Complete Correspondence III, Alliance Declining* (Norwalk, Conn.: Easton Press, 1995), p. 294.

29 Mikolajczyk, *Rape of Poland*, pp. 286–87.

30 Ibid., p. 82.

31 Hull, *Memoirs, Volume II*, pp. 1714–15.

32 Ibid., p. 1715.

33 Ibid.

34 George F. Kennan, *Memoirs 1925–1950* (Boston: Little, Brown and Company, 1967), p. 519.

35 Ibid., pp. 521–22.

36 Ibid., p. 529.

37 Ibid., pp. 522–23.

38 Harriman and Abel, *Special Envoy to Churchill and Stalin*, p. 367.

39 Ibid., p. 369.

40 Hull, *Memoirs, Volume II*, pp. 1715–16.

41 Henry A. Wallace, *The Price of Vision, The Diary of Henry A. Wallace 1942–1946* (Boston: Houghton Mifflin Company, 1973), p. 457.

42 Acheson, *Present at the Creation*, p. 88.

43 Charles E. Bohlen, *Witness to History 1929–1969* (New York: W. W. Norton and Company, 1973), p. 166.

44 Robert E. Sherwood, *Roosevelt and Hopkins, an Intimate History* (New York: Harper Brothers, 1948), p. 835.

45 Harriman and Abel, *Special Envoy to Churchill and Stalin*, p. 372.

46 John Morton Blum, *From the Morgenthau Diaries, Years of War 1941–1945,* (Boston: Hougton Mifflin Company, 1967), p. 392.

47 Edward R. Stettinius, *The Diaries of Edward R. Stettinius, Jr. 1943–1946,* edited by Campbell and Herring (New York: New Viewpoints, 1975), p. 184.

48 Ibid.

49 Ibid.

50 Ibid., p. 187.

51 Ibid., p. 201.

52 Ibid., p. 208.

53 Kimball, editor. *Churchill and Roosevelt III, Alliance Declining,* pp. 482–83.

54 Ibid., p. 484.

55 Eleanor Roosevelt, *This I Remember* (New York: Harper Brothers, 1949), pp. 253–54.

56 Ibid., p. 316.

57 Aleksandr Solzhenitsyn, *The First Circle* (New York: Harper & Row, 1968), pp. 101–02.

58 Aleksandr Solzhenitsyn, "Misconceptions About Russia are a Threat to America," vol. 58, no. 4, *Foreign Affairs,* Spring 1980, pp. 803–4.

59 Ibid., p. 806.

60 Ibid., p. 816.

61 Ibid., pp. 816–17.

62 Ibid., p. 818.

63 Ibid., p. 819.

64 Ibid., p. 821.

65 Ibid., pp. 833–34.

CHAPTER EIGHT

1 Lord Moran, *Churchill Taken from the Diaries of Lord Moran* (Boston: Houghton Mifflin, 1966), p. 242–43.

2 Winston S. Churchill, *The Second World War****** Triumph and Tragedy* (Boston: Houghton Mifflin, 1953), p. 397.

3 John Morton Blum, *From the Morgenthau Diaries, Years of War 1941–1945,* (Boston: Houghton Mifflin, 1967), p. 423.

4 Ross T. McIntire, *White House Physician* (New York: G. P. Putnam's Sons, 1946), p. 239.

5   Ibid., p. 15.

6   Ibid., p. 17.

7   Ibid., p. 239.

8   Ibid., p. 202.

9   Ibid., pp. 220–21.

10 Ernest K. Lindley, "Roosevelt: Sidelights and Appraisals," *Virginia Quarterly Review,* volume 23, number 1, winter 1947, p. 153.

11 Howard G. Bruenn, "Clinical Notes on the Illness and Death of President Franklin D. Roosevelt," *Annals of Internal Medicine,* vol. 72, no. 4, April 1970, p. 579.

12 Ibid., pp. 579–80.

13 Ibid., p. 580.

14 Ibid., p. 587.

15 Howard G. Bruenn, and Jan Kenneth Herman, "The President's Cardiologist," *Navy Medicine,* vol. 81, no. 2, March–April 1990, pp. 10–11.

BIBLIOGRAPHY

DIARIES AND LETTERS (AMERICAN)

Forrestal, James, *The Forrestal Diaries,* edited by Walter Millis, New York: Viking Press, 1951.

Hassett, William D., *Off the Record with FDR 1942–1945,* New Brunswick, NJ: Rutgers University Press, 1958.

Ickes, Harold L., *The Secret Diary of Harold L. Ickes, Volume III, Lowering Clouds 1939–1941,* New York: Simon and Schuster, 1954.

Kennedy, Joseph P., *Hostage to Fortune, the Letters of Joseph P. Kennedy,* edited by Amanda Smith, New York: Viking Penguin, 2001.

Morgenthau, Henry Jr., *From the Morgenthau Diaries, Years of War 1941–1945,* by John Morton Blum, Boston: Houghton Mifflin Company, 1967.

Stettinius, Edward R., *The Diaries of Edward R. Stettinius, Jr. 1943–1946,* New York: New Viewpoints, A Division of Franklin Watts, 1975.

Stilwell, Joseph W., *The Stilwell Papers,* arranged and edited by Theodore H. White, New York: William Sloan Associates, 1948.

Suckley, Margaret L., *Closest Companion,* edited and annotated by Geoffrey C. Ward, Boston: Houghton Mifflin Company, 1995.

Truman, Harry S., *Dear Bess, the Letters from Harry to Bess Truman 1910-1959,* edited by Robert H. Ferrell, New York: W. W. Norton & Company, 1983.

Wallace, Henry A., *The Price of Vision, The Diary of Henry A. Wallace 1942–1946,* edited by John Morton Blum, Boston: Houghton Mifflin Company, 1973.

DIARIES (BRITISH)

Alanbrooke, Field Marshal Lord, *Triumph in the West,* a history of the war years based on the diaries of Field Marshal Lord Alanbrooke, Chief of the Imperial General Staff by Arthur Bryant, New York: Doubleday & Company, 1959.

Cadogan, Sir Alexander, *The Diaries of Sir Alexander Cadogan 1938–1945,* edited by David Dilks, New York: G. P. Putnam's Sons, 1972.

Colville, John, *The Fringes of Power, 10 Downing Street Diaries 1939–1955,* New York: W. W. Norton Company, 1985.

MEMOIRS (AMERICAN)

Acheson, Dean, *Present at the Creation,* New York: W. W. Norton Company, 1969.

Barkley, Alben W., *That Reminds Me,* Garden City, NY: Doubleday & Company, 1954.

Baruch, Bernard M., *Baruch, the Public Years,* New York: Holt, Rinehart and Winston, 1960.

Biddle, Francis, *In Brief Authority,* Garden City, NY: Doubleday & Company, 1962.

Bohlen, Charles E., *Witness to History 1929–1969,* New York: W. W. Norton, 1973.

Byrnes, James F., *All in One Lifetime,* New York: Harper Brothers, 1958.

Catledge, Turner, *My Life and The Times,* New York: Harper & Row, 1971.

Flynn, Edward J., *You're the Boss,* New York: Viking Press, 1947.

Harriman, W. Averell and Abel, Elie, *Special Envoy to Churchill and Stalin 1941–1946,* New York: Random House, 1975.

Hull, Cordell, *The Memoirs of Cordell Hull, Volume I,* London: Hodder & Stoughton, 1948.

Hull, Cordell, *The Memoirs of Cordell Hull, Volume II,* New York: Macmillan, 1948.

Kennan, George F., *Memoirs 1925–1950,* Boston: Little, Brown and Company, 1967.

King, Ernest J. and Whitehill, Walter Muir, *Fleet Admiral King, A Naval Record,* New York: W. W. Norton & Company, 1952.

Lash, Joseph P., *Eleanor Roosevelt, A Friend's Memoir,* Garden City, NY: Doubleday & Company, 1964.

Leahy, William D., *I Was There,* New York: Whittlesey House, McGraw-Hill Book Company, 1950.

MacArthur, Douglas, *Reminiscences,* New York: McGraw-Hill Book Company, 1964.

McIntire, Ross T., *White House Physician,* New York: G. P. Putnam's Sons, 1946.

Murphy, Robert, *Diplomat among Warriors,* Garden City, NY: Doubleday & Company, 1964.

Perkins, Frances, *The Roosevelt I Knew,* New York: Viking Press, 1946.

Reston, James, *Deadline a Memoir,* New York: Random House, 1991.

Roosevelt, Eleanor, *This I Remember,* New York: Harper Brothers, 1949.

Roosevelt, Elliott, *As He Saw It,* New York: Duell, Sloan and Pearce, 1946.

Roosevelt, James and Shalett, Sidney, *Affectionately FDR, A Son's Story of a Lonely Man,* New York: Harcourt, Brace & Company, 1959.

Rosenman, Samuel I, *Working with Roosevelt,* New York: Harper Brothers, 1952.

Stimson, Henry L. and Bundy, McGeorge, *On Active Service in Peace and War,* New York: Harper Brothers, 1947.

Tames, George, *Eye on Washington, The Presidents Who Have Known Me,* New York: Harper Collins, 1990.

Truman, Harry S., *Memoirs by Harry S. Truman, Volume One, Year of Decisions,* New York: Doubleday & Company, 1958.

Tully, Grace, *FDR, My Boss,* New York: Charles Scribner's Sons, 1949.

MEMOIRS (BRITISH)

Churchill, Winston S., *The Second World War*** The Grand Alliance,* Boston: Houghton Mifflin Company, 1950.

Churchill, Winston S., *The Second World War**** The Hinge of Fate,* Boston: Houghton Mifflin Company, 1950.

Churchill, Winston S., *The Second World War****** Triumph and Tragedy,* Boston: Houghton Mifflin Company, 1953.

Cunningham, Viscount, *A Sailor's Odyssey,* New York: E. P. Dutton & Company, 1951.

Eden, Anthony, *The Memoirs of Anthony Eden, Earl of Avon, The Reckoning,* Boston: Houghton Mifflin Company, 1965.

Slim, Field Marshal the Viscount, *Defeat into Victory,* New York: David McKay Company, 1961.

Wheeler-Bennett, Sir John, *Special Relationships, America in Peace and War,* New York: St. Martin's Press, 1975.

OTHER MEMOIRS

Mikolajczyk, Stanislaw, *The Rape of Poland,* New York: McGraw-Hill Book Company, 1948.

BIOGRAPHIES (AMERICAN)

Adams, Henry A., *Harry Hopkins: A Biography,* New York: G. P. Putnam's Sons, 1977.

Alsop, Joseph, *FDR, 1882–1945, A Centenary Remembrance,* New York: Viking Press, 1982.

Buell, Thomas B., *Master of Sea Power, A Biography of Fleet Admiral Ernest J. King,* Boston: Little, Brown and Company, 1980.

Burns, James MacGregor, *Roosevelt, 1940–1945, The Soldier of Freedom,* New York: Harcourt Brace Jovanovich, 1970.

Freidel, Frank, *Franklin D. Roosevelt, A Rendezvous with Destiny,* Boston: Little, Brown and Company, 1990.

Goodwin, Doris Kearns, *No Ordinary Time, Franklin and Eleanor Roosevelt: The Home Front in World War II,* New York: Simon & Schuster, 1994.

McCullough, David, *Truman,* New York; Simon & Schuster, 1992.

McJimsey, George, *Harry Hopkins, Ally of the Poor and Defender of Democracy,* Cambridge, Mass.: Harvard University Press, 1987.

Sherwood, Robert E., *Roosevelt and Hopkins, an Intimate History,* New York: Harper Brothers, 1948.

Truman, Margaret, *Harry S. Truman,* New York: William Morrow & Company, 1973.

Tuchman, Barbara W., *Stilwell and the American Experience in China 1911-45,* New York: Macmillan, 1970.

BIOGRAPHIES (BRITISH)

Gilbert, Martin, *Winston S. Churchill, Volume VII, Road to Victory 1941–1945,* Boston: Houghton Mifflin Company, 1986.

Nicolson, Nigel, *Alex, The Life of Field Marshal Earl Alexander of Tunis,* New York: Atheneum, 1973.

Soames, Mary, *Clementine Churchill, The Biography of a Marriage,* Boston: Houghton Mifflin Company, 1979.

HISTORIES AND OTHER NONFICTION

Crispell, Kenneth R. and Gomez, Carlos F., *Hidden Illness in the White House,* Durham, NC: Duke University Press, 1988.

Dimbleby, David and Reynolds, David, *An Ocean Apart, The Relationship between Britain and America in the Twentieth Century,* New York: Random House, 1988.

Ferrell, Robert H., *Choosing Truman, The Democratic Convention of 1944,* Columbia: University of Missouri Press, 1994.

Ferrell, Robert H., *The Dying President Franklin D. Roosevelt 1944–1945,* Columbia: University of Missouri Press, 1998.

Ferrell, Robert H., *Ill-Advised Presidential Health and Public Trust,* Columbia: University of Missouri Press, 1992.

Franks, Norman, *Aircraft v. Aircraft, The Illustrated Story of Fighter Pilot Combat since 1914,* New York: Macmillan, 1986.

Macdonald, John, *Great Battles of World War II,* New York: Macmillan, 1986.

Ogburn, Charlton Jr., *The Marauders,* New York: Harper Brothers, 1956.

Pogue, Forrest C., *George C. Marshall Interviews and Reminiscences for Forrest C. Pogue,* Lexington, Virginia: George C. Marshall Research Foundation, 1991.

White, Theodore H. and Jacoby, Annalee, *Thunder Out of China,* New York: William Sloane Associates, 1946.

White, Theodore H., *In Search of History: A Personal Adventure,* New York: Harper & Row, 1978.

REFERENCE WORKS

American Chronicle, Six Decades in American Life 1920–1980, edited by Lois Gordon and Alan Gordon, New York: Atheneum, 1987.

American Testament, Fifty Great Documents of American History, edited by Irwin Glusker and Richard M. Ketchum, New York: American Heritage Publishing Co., 1971.

Blood, Toil, Tears, & Sweat, The Speeches of Winston Churchill, edited by David Cannadine, Boston: Houghton Mifflin Company, 1989.

Churchill and Roosevelt, The Complete Correspondence, Volumes I, II, and III, edited with commentary by Warren F. Kimball, Norwalk, Conn.: Easton Press, 1995.

FDR's Fireside Chats, edited by Russell D. Buhite and David W. Levy, New York: Penguin Books, 1993.

The Mayors—The Chicago Political Tradition, edited by Paul M. Green and Melvin G. Holli, Carbondale: Southern Illinois University Press, 1995.

The Oxford Companion to World War II, general editor ICB Dear, Oxford: Oxford University Press, 1995.

The Supreme Court Justices Illustrated Biographies 1789–1993, edited by Clare Cushman, Washington, DC: Congressional Quarterly, 1993.

JOURNALS AND PERIODICALS

Bruenn, Howard G., "Clinical Notes on the Illness and Death of President Franklin D. Roosevelt," *Annals of Internal Medicine,* vol. 72, no. 4, April 1970.

Bruenn, Howard G., and Herman, Jan Kenneth, "Interview FDR's Cardiologist: Dr. H.G. Bruenn," *Navy Medicine,* vol. 81, no. 2, March–April 1990.

Lindley, Ernest K., "Roosevelt: Sidelights and Appraisals," *Virginia Quarterly Review,* volume 23, number 1, winter 1947.

Solzhenitsyn, Aleksandr, "Misconceptions About Russia Are a Threat to America," *Foreign Affairs*, volume 58, number 4, spring 1980.

UNPUBLISHED HISTORICAL DOCUMENTS

Press and Radio Conference by Admiral Ross T. McIntire on 8 June 1944, Stephen Early Collection, Box 42, 6/8/44, FDR Library, Hyde Park, NY.

Cable from Earl of Halifax to Foreign Office on 10 December 1944, Public Record Office, Kew, Richmond, Surrey, TW94DU, UK.

Cable from Prime Minister Churchill to Harry Hopkins, 11 December 1944, Public Record Office, Kew, Richmond, Surrey, TW94DU, UK.

Summary of telegrams for the president dated 17 November 1944 at 7:00 A.M., President's Secretary's Files Collection, Box No. 73, FDR Library, Hyde Park, NY.

Secretary of the Navy James Forrestal's diary entry for 17 November 1944, James Forrestal Papers, Seeley G. Mudd Manuscript Library, Princeton University, Princeton, NJ.

Cable from FDR to Chiang Kai-shek on 6 July 1944, Map Room Collection, Box No. 10, FDR Library, Hyde Park, NY.

Written Order from FDR to Brigadier General Patrick J. Hurley on 12 August 1944, President's Secretary's File, Box No. 138, FDR Library, Hyde Park, NY.

Cable from FDR to Chiang Kai-shek on 16 September 1944, Map Room Collection, Box No. 10, FDR Library, Hyde Park, NY.

Draft by General George C. Marshall of cable, not sent, from FDR to Chiang Kai-shek, Marshall Papers, Box 81, Folder 23, George C. Marshall Research Foundation, Lexington, VA.

Cable from Brigadier General Patrick J. Hurley to FDR on 13 October 1944, Map Room Collection, Box No. 11, FDR Library, Hyde Park, NY.

White House Usher's Diary for 15 November 1944, White House Office of Social Entertainments Collection, FDR Library, Hyde Park, NY.

White House Usher's Diary for 17 November 1944, White House Office of
    Social Entertainments Collection, FDR Library, Hyde Park, NY.

TELEPHONE INTERVIEWS

Three or more interviews with Dorothy Bruenn, widow of Howard G. Bruenn.
Two or more interviews with Robert Hopkins, son of Harry L. Hopkins.
One interview with Jean Douglas, daughter of Henry A. Wallace.
One interview with Thomas E. Dewey Jr., son of Thomas E. Dewey.
One interview with Eugene Casey, son of Eugene B. Casey.
One interview with Betsey Metz, daughter of Eugene B. Casey.

INDEX

A

A.B.D.A. (Americans, British, Dutch, and Australians) operations, 92–93
Acheson, Dean
    on Hull, 65, 122
    on Hurley, 69–70
    Lend Lease Stage II, 82
    on Stettinius, 136
    on Welles, 122
Addington, Linda, xv
Afghanistan, 142
Albany Medical College, 151
Alexander, Sir Harold
    in Burma (Myanmar), 95, 96–97
    Operation Overlord, 76–78
Algiers, 127
Allen, George E., 42
Alsop, Joseph, 101
Amalgamated Clothing Workers of America, 37
Andaman Islands, 103
Annals of Internal Medicine, 151
anti-Semitism, 39
Anvil operation, 75–78, 80
Arakan, 104
Arnold, Henry Harley (Hap), 98

Atkinson, Brooks, 115
Atlantic Charter, 74–75
atomic energy agreements, 81
Attlee, Clement, 82
Atwood, Bishop, 17–18
Australia, ambassador to, 40
aviation routes, postwar planning, 82–83
Azores, Portugal, 132–33

B

Balkans, 78
Bandoeng, Java, 92
Barkley, Alben, 37, 40, 44
Baruch, Bernard, 24–26, 49–50
    Ickes letter to, 49–50
Bataan Peninsula, 92
Battle of France, 52–53
Behrens, Charles, 23
Belloc, Hilaire, 39
Bessarabia, 133
Bethesda Naval Hospital
    FDR's medical center, xi–xii, 20, 22, 23, 33
    FDR's medical records at, 152, 155
    Hull at, 135
Biddle, Francis, 38

Biles, Roger, on Kelly, 38
Boettiger, Anna Roosevelt (Mrs. James
    Halsted)
    Bruenn's article on FDR's health,
        151, 153–55
    on FDR's health, 22, 28
    as FDR's hostess and daughter,
        17–18, 22, 25, 147, 148
    on FDR's views of VP selection, 45
Boettiger, Buzzie, 18, 22
Boettiger, John (husband of Anna), 22,
    42, 103, 147
Boettiger, Sistie, 18, 22
Bohlen, Charles E.
    on Hopkins, 52, 57
    on Polish-Soviet relations, 138–39
    on Stettinius, 136
    Teheran Conference, 57, 73–74
Bose, Subhas Chandra, 104
bosses, influence on VP selection, 5,
    37–50. see also Flynn, Edward J.;
    Hannegan, Robert E.; Kelly,
    Edward J.
Bremerton Navy Yard, Washington, 29
Bridges, Sir Edward, 87
Britain. see Great Britain
British Expeditionary Force (BEF), 52
Bronx, New York, boss. see Flynn,
    Edward J.
Brooke, Sir Alan, 77
Bruenn, Dorothy, xiv
Bruenn, Howard G., 146
    education and career, xi–xii, 22,
        149, 151
    as FDR's cardiologist, 4, 22, 23, 26,
        33, 147, 150
    on FDR's health in 1970 article,
        151–55
    FDR's Pacific tour, 28–30
    Herman's interview of, 153–55
    visits to FDR retreats, 25, 33, 153
Bukovina, 133
Bullitt, William C., 132

Burma (Myanmar)
    Burma Corps, 94–95, 97
    Burma Road, 92–93
    China-Burma-India theater, 92–116
    fall and march out by Stilwell,
        97–99
    Japanese invasion, 92–93, 96
    recapture by Allies, 99, 103–6
Butler, Pierce, 38
Byelorussia, 73
Byrd, Harry, 37
Byrnes, James F.
    FDR and, 35, 39–40, 47
    FDR on, 45, 137
    "Hold-the-Line Order," 43, 47
    as potential secretary of state, 136,
        137
    as potential VP, 43–49, 50
    transcript of FDR conversation,
        44–45

C

Cadogan, Sir Alexander, on Hull, 66
Cairo Conference (1943), 68, 102–3
Camp Pendleton, California, 28
Cardozo, Benjamin Nathan, 54
Caribbean cruise (1940), 54
Casablanca, French Morocco, 128
Casablanca Conference (1943), 19, 80
Caserta, Italy, 89
Casey, Betty Brown, 63–64
Casey, Eugene Bernard, 58, 61–64
Catholic vote, 43, 45
Catledge, Turner, on FDR's health,
    24–25, 31–32
Catoctin Mountains, Md., 26
CBI (China-Burma-India theater),
    94–116. see also Burma
    (Myanmar); China; India; Stilwell,
    Joseph Warren
Cermak, Anton, J., 37
Chamberlain, Neville, 122, 143
Chennault, Claire, as commander of

U.S. 14th Air Force, 94, 100–101, 102, 106, 108
Chiang Kai-shek
Cairo Conference, 103
Chennault and, 100–101
FDR and, 93, 100–101, 103, 113, 116
Hurley as intermediary, 107–8, 110–13
personal qualities, 93, 97, 99
Stilwell as commander of 5th and 6th Chinese Armies, 92–93, 94, 95, 97, 99
Stilwell as potential commander of all Chinese armies, 99, 106–13
Theodore White on, 115
Chiang Kai-shek, Madame, visit to U.S., 100–101
Chicago, Illinois
boss (see Kelly, Edward J.)
Democratic conventions (see Democratic Party)
political issues in, 37–38
China
ambassador to, 39–40
Chiang Kai-shek (see Chiang Kai-shek)
China-Burma-India theater, 93–116
postwar planning, 61, 68
Stilwell (see Stilwell, Joseph Warren)
5th and 6th Armies, 94, 95, 96, 97, 99–100
China-Burma-India theater (CBI), 94–116. see also Burma (Myanmar); China; India; Stilwell, Joseph Warren
Chungking Embassy, China, 112
Churchill, Clementine, 60
Churchill, Randolph, 148
Churchill, Sarah, 102, 148
Churchill, Sir Winston Leonard Spencer
Anvil operation, 75–78, 80
Battle of France, 52–53

China-Burma-India theater, 99, 103
on democracy and imperialism, 71
on Dunkirk, 53
Eleanor Roosevelt and, 60–61
FDR and, 5, 67–90, 73–75, 80–82, 89–90
on FDR's health, 30–31, 148
Greece guerilla conflict (E.L.A.S.), 84–90
on Hong Kong, 68
on Hopkins, 56–58, 67–68
Hopkins and, 55–58, 61, 64–66, 67–68, 85–86
"iron curtain," origin of phrase, 150–51
Katyn Forest Massacre, 117–20
Lend-Lease aid, 54–56, 80–82, 83, 89
on oil production in Middle East, 71–73
Polish-Soviet relationships, 73–75
postwar planning, 68, 71–75
Quebec Conference (1944), 15, 30, 57–58, 64, 80–82
Stalin and, 64, 73–75, 79–80
Warsaw Uprising, 78–80, 129–31
CIO, Political Action Committee, 37, 45
"Clinical Notes on the Illness and Death of President Franklin D. Roosevelt" by H. G. Bruenn, 151–55
colonialism, 68, 71
Colville, John (Jock), 67, 79, 81, 83
communism
E.L.A.S. guerilla conflict, 84–90
Kennan on, 133–34
Solzhenitsyn on, 141–43
congestive heart failure, 4
Conner, Dorothy, xi
Corregidor, Phillipines, 92
Cox, James, 36
Creel, George, as collaborator of White House Physician, 149

Crowley, Leo, 47
Cumberland Law School, Lebanon,
    Tennessee, 120
Cunningham, Sir Andrew Browne, 84
Curtin, John, 25
Curzon, Lord George Nathaniel, 73
Curzon Line, 73–75, 125, 126, 129

D

D-Day, 106
Daniels, Jonathan, 63
Davis, Vincent, xv
Delano, Laura, 60
Democratic National Committee, 37,
    39, 40, 46, 50, 62–63
Democratic Party Conventions, Chicago
    1940 Convention, 63
    1944 Convention, 28, 46–50, 63
Depression, 2–3
Dewey, Thomas E., 31
digitalis, 4, 23
Dillard, Hardy Cross, xiii
Dimapur, India, 105
Douglas, William O., 43, 44–45, 48–49
Dow Jones Industrial Average (1932), 2
Duncan, Robert, as FDR's physician, 23,
    33
Dunkirk, France, 53
Dutch East Indies, 92–93

E

Early, Stephen T., as FDR's press secre-
    tary, 19, 27, 29
East Indies, 92–93
Eden, Sir Anthony, Earl of Avon, 117,
    118, 125–26
Eisenhower, Dwight D., 75–76
E.L.A.S. (Peoples National Army of
    Liberation in Greece), 84–90
election, 1932, FDR's health informa-
    tion, 3
election, 1944

bosses, 37
Catholic vote, 43, 45
CIO, Political Action Committee,
    37
labor movement and VP selection,
    45–47
Negro vote, 38, 43, 45, 47
Polish American vote, 73–74, 129
England. see Great Britain

F

Farley, James A., 37
Ferdinand Magellan (Presidential railroad
    car), 28
Fine, Sidney, 38
Flynn, Edward J.
    as anti-Semite, 39
    Byrnes and, 46
    FDR and, 37, 39–40, 47
    FDR and Hopkins estrangement,
        63
    on Hannegan as DNC chair, 40
    Ickes on, 39, 50
    Truman's selection as VP, 35,
        42–43, 46, 63
    Wallace on, 39, 63
Formosa invasion plan, 29
Forrestal, James, 62, 89, 90
Fox, George, 33
France
    Anvil operation, 75–78, 80
    Battle of France, 52–53
    Operation Overlord, 75–78
Franklin D. Roosevelt Library, Hyde
    Park, New York, xv, 1, 20, 155

G

Galahad (Merrill's Marauders), 103–4
Gauss, Clarence, 112
George, Lloyd, 73
German-Russian Nonaggression Pact of
    1939, 133

Germany
  Adolf Hitler, 77, 78
  Battle of France, 52–53
  Katyn Forest Massacre, 117–20
  Nineteenth Army, 78
Grayson, Cary, 18–19
Great Britain
  aviation routes, postwar planning,
    82–83
  Battle of France, 52–53
  British Expeditionary Force (BEF),
    52
  China-India-Burma theater, 94–97,
    103, 106
  Churchill (see Churchill, Sir
    Winston Leonard Spencer)
  FDR's views on British imperialism,
    68
  Greece E.L.A.S. guerilla conflict,
    84–90
  Royal Navy, 84
Great Depression, 2–3
Greece, E.L.A.S. guerilla conflict, 84–90

H

Hague, Frank, 37, 63
Halifax, Lord, Edward Frederick Lindley
  Wood, E.L.A.S. guerilla conflict,
  85–87
Halsted, Anna. see Boettiger, Anna
  Roosevelt (Mrs. James Halsted)
Halsted, James, 151
Hannegan, Robert E.
  as DNC chair, 40–41, 46, 50
  role in selection of Truman, 41–43,
    44–45, 46–49
  Truman and, 36, 47–48
Harper, John, 23
Harriman, Kathleen, 123
Harriman, William Averell
  as ambassador to Soviet Union,
    119–20, 135
  as ambassador to U.S.S.R., 112–13

  on Hopkins' role in secretary of
    state appointment, 136
  Kennan's report on Soviet Union to,
    133–35
  Moscow Conference (1943), 123
  Teheran Conference, 73–74
Hassett, William D., on FDR's health,
  34
Hawaii, as part of Pacific Tour, 28–30
Haynes, Caleb, 98
Helvering, Guy T., 40
Henry, Frederick T., xiii
Herman, Jan Kenneth, as historian of
  FDR's health, xv, 153–55
Hewitt, H. Kent, E.L.A.S. guerilla con-
  flict, 84–86
Hillman, Sidney, role in VP selection,
  37, 46–47
Hilltop Cottage, 41, 45
Hitler, Adolf, 77, 78
Hobcaw, S.C., retreat for FDR, 24–26,
  152–53
Hold-the-Line Order, 43, 47
Hong Kong, China, 68, 92
Hopkins, Diana, 59
Hopkins, Harry Lloyd, 51–66
  Bohlen on, 52, 57
  Cairo Conference, 102–3
  Casey and FDR estrangement, 58,
    62–64
  Chennault and, 101
  Churchill and, 55–58, 61, 64–66,
    67–68, 85–86
  education and career, 51–54, 64
  Eleanor Roosevelt estrangement
    role, 58–61
  FDR advisor and friend, 5, 51–57,
    63, 64–65, 67, 68, 87, 89,
    148
  FDR estrangement, 5, 57–66
  Flynn and FDR estrangement, 63
  Greece guerilla conflict role
    (E.L.A.S.), 84–90

health of, 51–52, 54, 56, 58, 59
on his career, 1940, 53–54
Ickes feud, 65
on Madame Kai-shek, 100, 101
on McIntire's concerns about FDR's
     heart condition, 20
personal qualities, 52, 56, 59, 94
Quebec Conference (1944),
     absence, 57–58, 65, 80
residency at White House, 52, 59,
     62
Sherwood as biographer of, 58, 62,
     64
Stettinius' appointment as secretary
     of state, 136
Stilwell as potential commander of
     Chinese forces, 110–11
Stilwell on, 94
Teheran Conference (1943), 57
Wallace and FDR estrangement,
     62–63
Howe, Louis, 39
Hull, Cordell
     Acheson on, 65, 122
     Cadogan on, 66
     education and early career, 120–21
     FDR and, 127–28, 131–32
     health, 66, 128, 131–32, 135–36,
          139
     Katyn Forest Massacre, 119–20
     Moscow Conference (1943),
          122–28, 139
     personal qualities, 126, 128
     Polish-Soviet relationships, 125–26,
          128–31, 139, 144
     as potential VP, 37
     Quebec Conferences, 65–66, 131
     resignation as secretary of state,
          131–32, 135–37, 139
     secretary of state, 64, 66, 121,
          122–28
     on Stalin, 124, 127
     Welles and, 121–23
Hull, Ress, 120

Hull, William, 120
Hurd, Charles, on FDR's health, 26–28
Hurley, Patrick J.
     as ambassador to China, 112
     as intermediary for Stilwell and
          Chiang, 107–8, 110–13
     views on British imperialism, 68–71
Hyde Park, N.Y., 20, 26, 31, 33, 34, 41,
     44, 58, 60, 137–38

I

Ichi-go, 105–6
Ickes, Harold L.
     on Chicago politics, 38
     on Edward J. Flynn, 39, 50
     Hopkins feud with, 65
     on VP selection, 49–50
imperialism, 68–71
Imphal, India, 98, 104–5, 106
India, 94, 99–100, 104–6
Iran, 68, 69–70, 71–73
"Iron Curtain," origin of phrase, 150–51
Ismay, Sir Hastings Lionel, 87
Italy, Anvil operation, 75–78

J

Jackson, Robert H., 38
Jacobson, Eddie, 36
Jacoby, Annalee, 114
Japan
     China-Burma-India theater, 94, 96,
          99, 100, 102–6, 108, 113–14
     POWs treatment by, 96
     WW II beginnings, 92
Jewish vote, 39
Johansen, Terry, xv

K

Kai-shek, Chiang. see Chiang Kai-shek
Kaiser, Henry J., 42
Katyn Forest Massacre, 117–20

Keegan, John, 78
Kelly, C. Brian, xv
Kelly, Edward J.
    Chicago mayor, 37–38
    Hannegan as DNC Chair, 40
    role in Truman selection, 42,
        46–47, 48, 50, 63
Kennan, George Frost, on Soviet-
    American relations, 117, 132–35,
    139
Kennedy, Joseph P., 32, 54
Kesselring, Albrecht, 76–77, 78
King, Ernest J.
    FDR's Pacific tour, 29
    Greece guerilla conflict (E.L.A.S.),
        84–90
Kohima, India, 105
Kung, H. H., 110, 111
Kunming, China, 93, 100
Kweilin, China, 108, 113
Kwiatkowski, Donna, xv

L

labor movement and VP selection, 37,
    45–47
Lahey, Frank H., 23
Leahy, William D.
    on Eleanor Roosevelt and
        Churchill, 60–61
    FDR and, 25, 41, 108
    FDR's Pacific tour, 41, 46
    Greece guerilla conflict (E.L.A.S.),
        85–86
    on VP selection, 47
Ledo Road, 108
Lee, Roger, on FDR's health, 148
LeHand, Marguerite, 48
Lend Lease aid to Britain
    FDR estrangement from Hopkins
        and, 64–65
    initiation of, 54–56
    Stage II continuation, 65, 80–82,
        83, 89

Stettinius role, 136
Levy, Robert, 22
Lewis, John, 101
Lindley, Ernest K., 151
Liuchow, China, 113
Lothian, Lord, Philip Henry Kerr, 55
Lublin Committee, 138–39
Luce, Henry R., 114
Lucus, Scott, 37
Lungling, China, 108

M

MacArthur, Douglas, 15
    on FDR's health, 29
    FDR's Pacific tour, 28, 45–46
    Phillipines liberation plan, 29
MacVeagh, Lincoln, 89
Marshall, George C.
    career, 84
    D-Day, 106
    FDR and, 113
    on King, 84
    Stilwell and, 92, 93, 102, 106–11,
        113
Massie, Robert K., xiv
McIntire, Ross T., 145
    Churchill and, 30–31
    education and career, 18–19
    FDR's medical records disappear-
        ance, 151–52, 154–55
    as FDR's personal physician, 3–4,
        19, 20, 22–23, 25–30, 33
    Hull's resignation and, 135–36
    Morgenthau on McIntire's secrecy,
        148–49
    secrecy about FDR's health, 22–23,
        24, 26, 27–28, 31, 147–55
    White House Physician (1946), 3–4,
        149–51, 153–55
McKenzie, Carter Wills, xvi
Meiktila, China, 96–97
Merrill, Frank D., 103–4
Merrill's Marauders, 103–4, 106

Middle East, postwar planning, 71–73
Mikolajczyk, Stanislaw, 128–31
"Misconceptions About Russia Are a
    Threat to America," by
    Solzhenitsyn, 142–43
Missouri political machines, 36, 42
Molotov, V. M., at Moscow Conference
    (1943), 123–26, 139
Moran, Lord, Sir Charles Wilson, on
    FDR's health, 31, 148
Morgenthau, Elinor, 17–18
Morgenthau, Henry, Jr.
    on FDR's health, 148–49
    Lend Lease Stage II negotiations,
        80–82
    New Year's Eve party (1943), 17–18
    on Stettinius' appointment as secre-
        tary of state, 136–37
Moscow Foreign Ministers' Conference
    (1943), 122–28, 139
Mountbatten, Lord Louis, 108
Murphy, Frank, 38
Murphy, Robert, 127–28
Murray, Phil, 46
Mutaguchi, Renya, 104, 106
Myanmar. *see* Burma (Myanmar)
Myitkyina, Burma (Myanmar), 103,
    106, 108

N

Navy Medicine, 153
Negro vote, 38, 43, 45, 47
Nelson, Donald, 107, 113
New York Times, 24, 26–28
Nimitz, Chester W., *15,* 28, 29, 45
Normandy, France, 106

O

oil reserves, postwar planning, 71–73
O'Malley, Sir Owen, on Katyn Forest
    Massacre, 117–19
Operation Overlord, 75–78

P

Pacific tour by FDR (Hawaii, Alaska,
    1944), *15,* 28–30, 45–46
Parks, Robert, xv
Pauley, Edwin W., 42
Paullin, James A., 23
Pearl Harbor, 19, 92
Peltz, Mary, xi
Pendergast, T. J., 36, 42
Perkins, Frances, on FDR, 1
Perry, Lewis, Jr., xi–xii, xiv
Perry, Mary, xiv–xv
Phillipines, 29, 92
Pogue, Forrest C., 84
Poland
    Curzon Line, 73–75, 125, 126, 129
    government-in-exile, 118, 125–26
    Katyn Forest Massacre, 117–20
    Lublin Committee, 138–39
    Mikolajczyk as prime minister,
        128–31
    Polish Committee of National
        Liberation, 131
    Soviet relations, 73–75, 120,
        125–26, 128–29, 133,
        138–39, 144
    as US foreign policy failure, 5,
        143–44
    Warsaw Uprising, 78–80, 129–31
    WWII beginnings, 52, 143
Polish American vote, 73–74, 129
Portugal, 132–33
Pratt, Mrs. Harold, 17–18

Q

Quebec Conference (1943), 57, 65, 66,
    117
Quebec Conference (1944)
    Churchill, *15,* 30, 57–58, 64,
        80–82
    FDR and Churchill, 30, 64
    FDR at, 31, 80–82, 131, 153

Hopkins' absence from, 57–58, 65,
    80
Hull, 65–66, 131
Lend Lease negotiations, 80–82, 89

R

Ramgarh, India, 99–100
Rangoon, Burma (Myanmar), 94, 96, 97
Rayburn, Sam, 37
Red Cross, 118
Reston, James (Scotty), 25
Roman Catholic vote, 43, 45
Rome, Italy, 75
Roosevelt, Anna. *see* Boettiger, Anna
    Roosevelt
Roosevelt, Eleanor
    Churchill and, 60–61
    FDR's health and, 21, 25
    on FDR's views of Stalin, 140–41
    Hopkins and, 58–61
    on Madame Kai-shek, 100–101
    postwar planning, 60, 61
    Wallace and, 60
    as wife and First Lady, 17–18, 21,
        25, 33, 58–59, 100–101, 147
Roosevelt, Elliott
    on FDR's involvement in Greek
        guerilla conflict affair
        (E.L.A.S.), 87–88
    on FDR's support for Stilwell,
        102–3
    role in FDR's administration,
        68–69
Roosevelt, Franklin D., as President
    Anvil operation, 75–78, 80
    Cairo Conferences, 68, 102–3
    Caribbean cruise (1940), 54–55
    Chiang Kai-shek and, 93, 100–101,
        103, 107–109, 113, 116
    Churchill and, 5, 64, 66, 71,
        73–75, 80–82, 84–88, 89–90
    Depression and, 2–3

education and early career, 35
first airplane flight (1943), 19–20
Flynn and, 37, 39–40, 47, 63
Greece guerilla conflict (E.L.A.S.),
    84–90
Hopkins as advisor, 5, 51–57, 63,
    64–65, 67, 68, 87, 89, 148
Hopkins estrangement, 5, 57–66
Hull as secretary of state, 122–28
Hull's resignation, 131–32, 135–36
on imperialism, 68
Katyn Forest Massacre, 117–20
Leahy as friend and advisor, 41
Lend-Lease aid, 54–56, 80–82, 83,
    89
Madame Kai-shek and, 101
New Year's Eve gathering, 1943,
    17–18
Pacific tour (1944), *15,* 28–30, 41,
    45–46
photographs of, 3, *6–16,* 29, 30,
    148
Polish-Soviet relationships, 73–75,
    129–31, 137–39
postwar planning, 68, 71–73, 128
Quebec Conference (1944), 30, 31,
    64, 80–82, 131, 153
on reelection in 1944, 41–42, 73
reelection in 1944, 28, 31–34
Soviet-American relationship views,
    127, 140
Stalin and, 5, 64, 73–75, 140–41
State Department relationship,
    68–69, 114, 126, 136–37,
    138–39
State of the Union address, 20, 138
Stilwell and, 5, 93, 102–3, 106–16
Truman's VP selection process,
    36–50
visits to Hobcaw, 25–26, 152–53
visits to Hyde Park (*see* Hyde Park,
    N.Y.)
visits to Shangri-La, 26

visits to Warm Springs, 33, 87, 137,
    148, 153
Wallace and, 36–37, 43–44, 45, 49
Warsaw Uprising, 78–80, 129–31
Roosevelt, Franklin D., health and med-
    ical treatment
adrenaline as sinus treatment, 19
alcohol use, 18
altitude restrictions, 19–20
angina pectoris, 30, 150
autopsy (not held), 155
blood pressure (hypertension), 3, 4,
    22, 31, 33, 152–53
bronchial pneumonia, as rumor, 27
bronchitis, 22, 27, 152
Bruenn as cardiologist (see Bruenn,
    Howard G.)
cardiovascular disease, 3, 18, 22,
    30, 33, 149, 152
cardiovascular disease treatment, 4,
    22–23
cerebral hemorrhage, 148
codeine, 23
congestive heart failure, 4, 148
cyst removal, 20
death, 148, 155
digitalis, 4, 23
enlarged heart, 3, 22, 149, 152
exercise, 18
gallstones, 25, 152
gastrointestinal tract, 23, 25, 27,
    28–29
on his doctors' withholding infor-
    mation, 25–26
inability to concentrate, 24–25, 148
influenza, 3, 20, 27
irritability, 148
kidneys, 4
knowledge of own health condition,
    23–24, 26, 28, 156
liver, 4, 148
McIntire as personal physician (see
    McIntire, Ross T.)
medical records, 3

medical records disappearance,
    151–52, 154–55
paralysis of lower limbs, 3
poliomyelitis, 2–3, 18
rest, 23, 26, 154
salt intake reduction, 23
sinus, 19, 27
sleeping patterns, 23, 148
stroke, 148
tobacco use, 4, 18, 23
weight, 3, 23, 24, 31
Roosevelt, James
on FDR's health, 17, 29
FDR's Pacific tour, 28–29
on FDR's privacy, 1
on VP selection, 49
Rosenman, Samuel I., *146*
FDR's Pacific tour, 46
on VP selection, 47–48
Russell, Theodore, xii
Russia. see U.S.S.R.
Ryan, Philip Henry, Jr., xvi

                        S

Salazar, Antonio, 132–33
Sato, Major General, 105
Saudi Arabia, postwar planning for, 72
Scott, Robert, 98
Sellers, Dilworth P., xv
Shangri-La (FDR's retreat in Md.), 26
Sherwood, Robert E.
Churchill interviews, 64
on Eleanor Roosevelt, 58
on FDR, 1–2
on FDR and Hopkins, 51, 64–65
as Hopkins' biographer, 58, 62, 64
on Stettinius, 136
Short, Walter C., 112
Shwebo, Burma (Myanmar), 97
Siam (Thailand), 96
Slim, William
China-Burma-India theater, 95, 96,
    97, 105, 106

Stilwell and, 95–96, 97, 98,
    99–100
Solzhenitsyn, Aleksandr, on Stalin,
    141–43
Spanish Civil War, 60
Spellman, Francis Joseph, 32
Springwood, N.Y., as FDR's estate. *see*
    Hyde Park, N.Y.
Stage II Lend Lease aid, 65, 80–82, 83,
    89, 136
Stalin, Joseph
    Churchill and, 64, 73–75, 79–80
    Curzon Line, 73, 129
    FDR and, 5, 64, 73–75, 140–41
    Hull on, 124, 127, 139
    Kennan on, 134
    Moscow Conference (1943),
        122–28, 139
    Polish-Soviet relationships, 73–75,
        120, 125–26, 129–31,
        138–39
    Solzhenitsyn on, 141–43
    Warsaw Uprising, 78–80, 129–31
Stark, Lloyd C., 36
Stettinius, Edward R., Jr.
    education and early career, 136,
        137
    on Lend Lease Stage II, 81–82, 136
    as secretary of state, 137–39
Stilwell, Joseph Warren, 91–116
    on British, 95
    Burma march out by, 97–99
    Burma recapture, 99, 103–6
    Chiang Kai-shek and, 92, 93, 99,
        111
    China-Burma-India theater com-
        mander, 112
    education and career, 91–92, 112
    FDR and, 5, 93, 102–3, 106–16
    on Hopkins, 94
    Hopkins and, 110–11
    Hurley as intermediary, 107–8,
        110–12

Marshall and, 92, 93, 102, 106–11,
    113
personal qualities of, 95–96, 98, 99,
    103
as potential commander of all
    Chinese armies, 106–14
relief from duties, 110, 112, 115
Slim and, 95–96, 97, 98, 99–100
Stimson and, 93
Theodore White on, 115
Wallace on, 113
Stimson, Henry L., 91, 93, 114
Suckley, Margaret
    on FDR's health, 20–21, 26, 30, 33
    on FDR's statements about reelec-
        tion, 41–42
    on FDR's statements about VP
        selection, 45
    relationship with FDR, 17–18,
        20–21, 25–26, 33

T

Tames, George, 30
Tammany Hall, 39
Teheran Conference (1943)
    Curzon Line, 129
    FDR and Churchill, 30, 78
    Hopkins at, 57
    McIntire on FDR's health, 4
    Polish-Soviet relationships, 73–75
    postwar planning, 68
Thompson, Malvina, 17–18
Tientsin, China, 92
Time-Life, 114
Treaty of Riga, 73
Trident Conference (1943), 101
Truman, Harry S., 35–50
    education and career, 36
    FDR and, 30, 35, 42–45, 47
    on FDR's health, 30, 32
    Hannegan and, 36, 41, 44
    Lend Lease termination, 82
    on own VP nomination, 44, 48

VP selection process and, 35–50
    (see also Vice-President, selec-
        tion of FDR's)
TUBE ALLOYS (atomic energy), 81
Tully, Grace, 21, 46, 48
Tydings, Millard, 37

U

U.S. Armed Forces
    8th Air Force, 79
    14th Air Force, 100–101
    5307th Composite Unit, 103
    5th Marine Division, 28
U.S. State Department
    FDR's tension with, 68–69
    Hopkins as secretary of state (see
        Hopkins, Harry Lloyd)
    Hull as secretary of state (see Hull,
        Cordell)
    Kennan on Soviet-American rela-
        tions, 132–35
    Poland as foreign policy failure, 5,
        139–40, 143–44
    Stettinius as secretary of state (see
        Stettinius, Edward R., Jr.)
U.S.S. Baltimore, 15
U.S.S. Cummings, 30, 150
U.S.S. Tuscaloosa, 54
U.S.S.R.
    Katyn Forest Massacre, 117–20
    Kennan on Soviet-American rela-
        tions (1944), 132–35
    Moscow Conference (1943),
        122–28, 139
    Polish relations, 73–75, 125–26,
        128–31, 133, 138–39
    postwar planning, 61
    Solzhenitsyn on, 141–43
    Stalin (see Stalin, Joseph)
    Warsaw Uprising, 78–80, 129–31

V

Vandenberg, Arthur, 137–38
Vice-President, selection of FDR's,
    35–50
    bosses, influence on VP selection, 5,
        37–50
    Byrnes as potential VP, 43–49, 50
    Flynn role (see Flynn, Edward J.)
    Hannegan role (see Hannegan,)
    Hillman role, 37, 46–47
    Hull as potential VP, 37
    Kelly role (see Kelly, Edward J.)
    labor movement and, 37, 45–47
    Truman as chosen VP (see Truman,
        Harry S.)
    Wallace as potential VP (see
        Wallace, Henry A.)
"Vinegar Joe." see Stilwell, Joseph
    Warren

W

Waccamaw River, S.C., 24
Walker, Frank, 42, 44–45, 63
Wallace, Henry A.
    on Casey and Hopkins, 61–63
    education and career, 36–37
    on Eleanor Roosevelt and
        Churchill, 60
    FDR on, 43–44, 45, 49
    on FDR's view of Stilwell's recall,
        113
    on Flynn, 39, 63
    on Hull's resignation, 136
    as potential secretary of state, 137
    as potential VP in 1944, 41, 42–43,
        46, 48–49, 63
    on Stilwell, 113
    as VP, 37, 43–44, 62
War Productions Board, 107
Warm Springs, Ga., 33, 87, 137, 148,
    153

Warsaw Uprising, 78–80, 129–31
Watson, Edwin M., 19, 25, 26
Wavell, Sir Archibald, 92
Welles, Sumner, 120–23
White, Theodore H., 114–15
White House Physician, by Ross T.
    McIntire, 149–51, 153–55
Wilderstein, estate of M. Suckley, 20, 30
Wills, George S., xv
Wills, Jesse Ely, xiii
Wills, Julia Ryan, xvi
Wills, Ridley, xiv
Wilson, Sir H. Maitland, 89
Wilson, Woodrow, ill health of, 4, 31,
    153
Winant, John, 82–83, 119, 148
World War II
    A.B.D.A. (Americans, British,
        Dutch and Australians), 92
    Anvil operation, 75–78, 80
    Atlantic Charter, 74
    beginnings in Europe, 52
    beginnings in Pacific, 92
    China-Burma-India theater, 92–116
    Greece guerilla conflict (E.L.A.S.),
        84–90
    Katyn Forest Massacre, 117–20
    "miracle of deliverance" at Dunkirk,
        53
    Operation Overlord, 75–76
    Polish-Soviet relationships (*see*
        Poland)
    postwar planning, 64, 68, 71–75,
        82–83, 123
    Solzhenitsyn on, 141–43
    Warsaw Uprising, 78–80, 129–31

Y

Yalta Conference, 147–48